THE *southern* SLOW COOKER

THE *southern* SLOW COOKER

Big-flavor, low-fuss recipes for comfort food classics

KENDRA BAILEY MORRIS

Photography by **ERIN KUNKEL**

TEN SPEED PRESS
BERKELEY

FOR *Tim*

Contents

Acknowledgments

It truly does take a village to create a cookbook, and I'll go one step further and add that it also takes church socials, barn raisings, family reunions, corn shuckins, tent revivals, and all day sing-alongs to get the job done. Basically, it takes the generous love and support of an outstanding community of family, friends, and colleagues. Without question, this book would not have been possible without the help and encouragement of many amazing folks.

Let me begin by thanking all the great folks at Ten Speed Press: my editors Julie Bennett and Emily Timberlake, as well as photographer Erin Kunkel and food stylist Katie Christ, who made my family recipes look prettier than I ever could. I would also like to thank my brilliant copyeditor, Andrea Chesman, for giving this manuscript a much-needed look-through.

To my recipe testers, thank you from the bottom of my heart. You were kind enough to donate your kitchens, slow cookers, and bellies to help make this book possible. Jason and Amy Tesauro, Matt Sadler (aka the Marinara), Jenna Helwig, Michelle Sharp, Heather Anne Stalker and the Churchill Gang: Karol and Chip Tompkins, Melissa Gropman, Courtney Lafond, Christopher Tompkins, Nathalie Molliet-Ribet, LaDonna Austin, and Katie Smith. To my amazing and hard-working extended family who cooked, tasted, and cooked again: my mother-in-law, Kathy Dalesandro, her husband Jorge Lober (sorry I made you fat), and my sister-in-law, Jessica; my father-in-law, Tom Morris (for giving up his freezer space and his belly); my brother-in-law, Jeff Morris, and his wife Ashley (and her brother, Barry, for eating all those ribs). Thank you.

In keeping with all things Southern, I must extended my deepest gratitude to my family: my grandmothers, Granny Boohler and Granny Belcher back in West Virginia for sharing with me their love of Appalachian cooking along with many handwritten and oral recipes that I will cherish forever. I must also thank my Aunt Barbara in Fairmont, West Virginia, for keeping the DeMary Italian cooking spirit alive and well through her West Virginia chili slaw dogs and Sunday gravy and pasta.

To my father, who has inspired me both as a writer and an artist, but most of all, who has taught me by example to simply be a better person in this world: Thank you. To my mother, who is my constant culinary inspiration, friend, and an expert recipe developer in her own right: You are the only person I know who can make the best tasting slow-cooked buttermilk chocolate cake, homemade apple butter, and slow-cooked corn pudding, all at the same time, while still looking 100 percent fabulous. Thank you for everything. I could not have done this without you.

Finally, to my husband, Tim: Thank you for hanging in there with me during this crazy journey. You never complained, even when our nightly dinners consisted of hot soups and stews during a sweltering 100°F Southern summer. Thank you for coming along on this wild ride. I know there'll be many more, and that makes me happy, because I'll get to travel with you.

Introduction

Here's to the legacy of Southern food. This is the good stuff, the kind of cooking that's built from family tradition and treasured, the scribbled-upon heirloom recipes passed down from mothers to daughters. Unquestionably, Southern food and cooking is experiencing a renaissance. Soul-satisfying, comfort food favorites like slow-simmered collards greens, flash-fried chicken, creamy grits, and light-as-air fresh rolls have become de rigueur in many restaurants throughout the country, and for good reason.

But what is Southern food?

Southern food is the welcome table, a convivial place where you can savor a hearty meal cooked with love and where there's always room for one more chair. It doesn't matter whether you're born and bred, a transplant, or just passing through: you are welcome here.

Southern food is a celebration, from eating a simple pulled pork barbecue 'n' slaw sandwich in the parking lot of a roadside joint to dressing the part (large red hats encouraged) for an elaborate Sunday supper of glazed ham, English peas, hot biscuits, and deviled eggs, complete with a pitcher of sweet tea.

Southern cooking is seasonal. Spring brings us butter beans, morels, ramps, and lamb. During the summer, fresh ears of sweet corn, fried green tomatoes, and fruit pies like blackberry and peach take center stage. Fall gives us briny oysters, warm churned apple butter, persimmons, and freshly slaughtered hogs that will eventually morph into bacon, ham, sausages, lard, and seasonings such as fatback and ham hocks. The first cold spell offers many of these delicacies all over again, but this time it's from our basements and pantries in the form of canned green beans, pickled beets, corn relishes, and sweet jams.

When it comes to cooking, cast-iron pots, Dutch ovens, and giant kettles set over fire are commonplace, especially when making food the low and slow way; for Southern folk, this is our way of life. From bubbling pots of sausage and duck gumbo at the annual Creole music festival to "wash-day" meals of red beans and rice with smoked sausage to Virginia Brunswick stew, Kentucky Burgoo, low-country chicken bogs, and black-eyed peas cooked with Sunday supper's ham bone, the one-pot, slow-cooked meal is an iconic symbol of the South.

Not surprisingly, down-home Southern cooking is simply made for the slow cooker. This is family-pleasing, comfort food at its finest. Think of stick-to-your-ribs classics like saucy bourbon-and-cola country-style ribs; Dr. Pepper baked ham; fall-off-the-bone chicken and dumplings; tender, glazed meatloaf; perfectly seasoned greens; sorghum syrup sweet potatoes; country ham bread pudding; and beans of all shapes and sizes. Even homemade desserts can be made in the slow cooker, and you can make them from scratch, the old-fashioned way, without resorting to boxed cake mixes or other processed ingredients. Sweet treats like warm chocolate spice cake, steamed banana pudding cheesecakes (baked in canning jars), glazed peach upside-down cake, and spiced molasses gingerbread come out sweet and dreamy in the slow cooker. How cool is that?

As I developed and tested the recipes for this book, I came away pleasantly surprised at how fantastic the slow cooker is when it comes to making some of my family's tried-and-true favorites. Not only did the "set it and forget it" concept leave me full days and afternoons for other tasks, but considering I wrote this book over the summer during a sweltering Southern heat wave, I can attest that my kitchen remained delightfully cool all day long, making me a newfound convert to the joys of slow cooking all year-round.

When it comes to time saving, the slow cooker can be your best friend. You'll note that most of the recipes in this book have long cooking times (6 to 8 hours or more), and this was deliberate on my part. I sought to create recipes that can be prepped and added to the slow cooker in the morning and then left to cook most of the day, so when you return home, a finished meal awaits along with a kitchen filled with delightful aromas. I can think of no easier way to get dinner on the table after a busy day.

As far as recipes go, the ones in this book are family favorites that I've adapted for slow cooking. In true Southern cooking form, they use primarily fresh and natural ingredients. This is not a book that relies on processed foods, mixes, or canned soups for thickeners or flavors because that's not how I was taught to cook by my elders. Instead, my family meals were filled with fresh-from-the-garden vegetables and meats from the farm based on seasonal availability. I've done my best to honor this style of cooking with the recipes contained in this book. However, I will offer this disclaimer: I do have two recipes that require condensed tomato soup, and you might find a bit of shortening and a tater tot or two in here, because sometimes you've got to live a little.

On that note, you'll also see that most of the recipes in the book have a suggested beverage pairing, which ranges from beer and wine to cocktails and sweet tea. These beverage pairings represent some of the best that local brewers, winemakers, cider makers, and mixologists from various parts of the South have to offer.

Southern food is something the home cook is proud to bring to her table and feed her family. As a result, some of these recipes require extra steps, such as pan searing meats and vegetables or making a butter/flour mixture to use as a thickener. You'll have to trust me when I say that these extra steps make the end results totally worth the effort. And maybe somewhere, your granny is smiling because you made her recipe just the way she likes it.

Using the Slow Cooker

Slow cookers, especially in the Southern kitchen, have stood the test of time, more than forty years, in fact. I remember my mom breaking out her vintage Rival, a 5-quart round cooker bearing the tell-tale colors of the 1970s: avocado and brown. She'd make everything from pinto beans to apple butter in it, and no matter what she was whipping up, the house always smelled divine.

Slow cookers are not only incredibly efficient, but they can also make typically laborious cooking tasks, such as making homemade chicken stock, a breeze. The cooker's gentle, low heat is simply made for breaking down tough cuts of meat like ribs, roasts, and shoulders until they are meltingly tender. And who knew you could bake a cake in the slow cooker? Well, you can, and it can be 100 percent homemade.

One of the best features of the slow cooker is that it can be left unattended for long periods of time, letting you take care of other business while the cooker does all the work. Also, even though some of the recipes in this book have less than six hours of cooking time (such as desserts and some side dishes), many do require longer cooking times and are, therefore, appropriate for prepping before you head off to work or to bed.

Choosing a Slow Cooker

Slow cookers come in various shapes and sizes, from 2-quart mini cookers that are perfect for dips and sauces to 7-quart slow cookers designed for oversized roasts or feeding a crowd. Slow cookers are either round or oval, and while there doesn't seem to be much difference between the two, I prefer oval-shaped cookers because they fit larger cuts of meat more easily.

There are several factors you should consider when choosing a slow cooker. If you are cooking for just two, purchasing a 4-quart model might be best; otherwise you might get stuck with too many leftovers. If your family is larger, I suggest going with a 6-quart model, which can serve anywhere from six to ten people, depending on the recipe. I've also found that a 5-quart model is a good middle-of-the-road choice and is highly versatile when it comes to cooking meats, sides, and desserts.

All of the recipes in this book were tested in a 5- or 6-quart slow cooker. However, most of them can be halved if you've got a smaller cooker, and nearly all of the final dishes and leftovers can be frozen easily. When developing the recipes for this book, I used three different slow cookers, each of which offered its own unique features.

My 5-quart was a manual Hamilton Beach Stay or Go oval slow cooker, a reasonably priced cooker that is large enough to hold a whole chicken, but small enough for cooking desserts and sides. It is portable with a lock-tight lid, so you can easily take it to a potluck.

I also used a programmable, oval KitchenAid 6-quart slow cooker with a hinged lid. The hinged lid allows you to give your food a stir without losing as much heat as with a standard lid. This model also has four settings: warm, low, medium and high.

My high-end cooker was a 6.5-quart programmable All-Clad slow cooker. Like the KitchenAid, it automatically sets to warm once it's done cooking, which is great if you're not able to make it home in time because it keeps the food at a safe, warm temperature. All-Clad also makes a slow cooker with a stovetop-friendly insert for browning the ingredients.

In the end, you should pick a slow cooker that fits your needs—will you be hauling it around to events? If so, invest in a locking lid. Will you be feeding a crowd? Opt for a bigger model. The one universal piece of advice I can offer is to look for a slow cooker with a removable insert (preferably ceramic): it will make cleanup much, much easier.

Cooking Tips

Most of the recipes in this book will serve six to eight people, with some serving more (Southerners love to feed people!). However, many recipes can be cut in half and cooked in a smaller slow cooker, if needed. Never fill your slow cooker more than two-thirds full, or the food may not cook safely and evenly. Conversely, if your slow cooker is filled less than half full, its contents will cook more quickly, so plan accordingly.

Be sure to take a moment to read through the recipe completely before starting. Since slow cookers vary by size, shape, model, heat settings (low versus high), and age (older slow cookers tend to run cooler than newer ones, for example), I've given approximate cooking times for each recipe.

I can't stress enough how important it is to know your slow cooker. Does it cook evenly or run hot? You'll find that most of the recipes in this book offer a range of cooking times. If your slow cooker *does* run hot, start checking for doneness on the early side; and then keep checking every thirty minutes or so. Do keep in mind that every time you lift the lid to check or stir (which is not prohibited, by the way), it adds to your cooking time, as much as twenty minutes. The temperature of your ingredients will affect cooking time as well. Did you toss in a chicken straight from the fridge or did you brown the meat first? All of these factors need to be considered when using the slow cooker.

Thoughts on Browning

For certain dishes to really shine (such as roasts, meatballs, or aromatic vegetables), browning the ingredients before slow cooking makes all the difference. Not only does this additional step concentrate the flavor of the food, but it creates a lovely char that's visually appealing, especially if you use a cast-iron pan, which is my personal choice (and the traditional Southern way to do it!).

That Dreaded Condensation

One of the biggest challenges when using the slow cooker is ending up with a surplus of extra liquid. By design, the slow cooker cooks with moist heat. However, this can backfire when you end up with watery chili. Condensed soups or cornstarch blends are often added as thickeners, but I prefer to keep these to a minimum since condensed soups are often high in sodium, and I've found that cornstarch can cause sauces and stews to become too thick. I prefer to thicken my sauces the old-fashioned way, by reducing them with the lid of the slow cooker taken off or set ajar. I've also had success incorporating a simple thickener made from a combination of butter and flour, which is called a *beurre-manie*. A *beurre-manie* is similar to a roux; however, unlike a traditional roux (which is cooked as part of the recipe), this is a simple room-temperature mixture of equal parts flour and butter that's whisked right into the pot. When making desserts such as cakes or cobblers, I've found that draping a thick layer of paper towels over the inside of the slow cooker works like a charm to absorb excess evaporation. After several hours, your paper towels may get soggy—in that case, just replace them with a fresh batch and continue to cook according to the recipe.

The Importance of Seasoning

Since slow cookers steam food for long periods of time, flavors can become diluted. Don't be afraid to season generously, especially toward the end of cooking. Seasonings such as fresh garlic, dried herbs, and hot peppers do wonders for a slow-cooked meal, and if you're going to add mostly fresh herbs, be sure to toss them in during the last thirty minutes or so. The exception to this rule is with heartier herbs, such as rosemary, which can hold up to longer cooking times. I also prefer to use broth in place of water for many recipes, since slow cooking already has the tendency to dilute flavors. Don't forget that naturally acidic foods, such as tomatoes or citrus, can act as tenderizers, so take this into consideration with regard to texture and cooking time. Finally, taste, taste, and taste some more, especially toward the end of cooking, and adjust seasonings accordingly, especially the salt and black pepper.

A Quick Note on Fats

No one wants to open up their slow cooker only to discover a thick layer of grease, so many recipes include removing additional visible fats from meats or poultry. This helps to make your dish healthier and prevents the meat from rendering too much fat.

Essential Kitchen Tools

Cast-Iron Pan

Southern cooks can't live without their cast-iron pans, and we use them often because they just get better with age. A well-seasoned cast-iron skillet provides a high-heat sear and gorgeous caramelization like nothing else, so I recommend investing in one for the browning required for these recipes. A 10- or 12-inch round cast-iron skillet that's about 2 inches deep, such as one made by Lodge Logic, is a good basic starter skillet. Not only is it a good buy, but it comes preseasoned.

Canning Jars

There is clearly a canning renaissance going on these days with home cooks "putting up" more than ever. The last chapter of this book features recipes that are great for home canning, and I've even got two where you cook your food in jars set right in the slow cooker. There are several styles and brands of canning jars out there to choose from, and they are now regularly available at most grocery stores, hardware stores, and online.

A PINCH OF THIS AND A SCOOP OF THAT
Southern cooking is not an exact science

I remember once asking my mom how much sugar went into her homemade apple butter recipe to which she answered, "Depends on the sweetness and size of your apples. It's not an exact science." Over the years, I would hear this phrase in all of its ambiguous glory applied to many family recipes, from the size of the piece of fatback that gets tossed into a pot of brown beans to the amount of raisins I should add to the applesauce cake batter.

Southern cooking can be frustratingly simplified sometimes.

Down-home Southern recipes are well-known to forgo teaspoons and cups in favor of pinches, smidgens, globs, spoonfuls, and handfuls. In fact, I can honestly say that I don't think I ever saw my granny use a measuring cup. She cooked with her eyes, her nose, her hands, and she tasted, tasted, tasted, adding a little more salt here and a handful of extra flour there until it was "right."

You might notice that some of the recipes in this book call for an inexact amount of sugar, salt "to taste," or a "pinch" of cayenne. This is not meant to befuddle or frustrate you; it is designed to provide you with options based on variation in ingredients (as with the size and natural sugar content of apples or peaches, for example). Cooking is a matter of taste, so add more or less seasonings as you see fit. Also, I can't stress enough how important it is to taste your food before it hits the table. This is a crucial and often overlooked step that can mean the difference between an average-tasting, under-seasoned dish and a stellar, memorable one.

Finally, some recipes in the book call for the addition of bacon fat or grease, which I've listed as optional. While bacon grease or other meaty seasonings unquestionably add a very Southern flair, they may not be appropriate for everyone's diet, so feel free to substitute vegetable or canola oil.

Parchment Paper and Cooking Spray

Anything nonstick can be your friend when it comes to slow cooking since it makes for easy clean-up, and I've found that parchment paper is a great asset. Parchment paper is virtually foolproof for releasing food, especially items of a sticky nature. I also recommend getting a can of cooking spray, such as canola or vegetable oil, and being generous with it when spraying the inside of your cooker. Not only does it help to prevent food from sticking, but it makes for minimal pot scrubbing at the end of the day.

A Baking Dish That Fits into Your Slow Cooker

A few of the dessert recipes in the book involve using a baking dish inside the slow cooker. You might think this is a bit superfluous, but I've found that cooking cake batter in a dish set inside the cooker makes for more even cooking and easier clean-up. For some recipes, it also prevents burning around the edges. Since slow cookers vary in shape and size, using a baking dish helps to keep the batter from either spreading out too much or filling a smaller slow cooker to capacity.

Sweet Southern Seasonings

A well-balanced Southern breakfast—a table spread with eggs, biscuits, fried apples, and cream gravy—is almost always served with pitchers of honey, sorghum syrup, and molasses. These particular syrups, as well as sugar and cola, can also be a home cook's best asset. As such, you'll see them pop up in many of the recipes in this book.

Sorghum Syrup

Drizzle a little of this sweet goodness over a buttered biscuit (with lots of butter, trust me on this one) and your eyes just might roll back up in your head: it's that good. Made from sorghum cane (not sugar cane), this light brown or amber-colored syrup results from slow cooking the juice extracted from sorghum stalks in an open pot until it turns into a thickened syrup. While sorghum syrup is good enough to eat with a spoon, it's often used to make homemade candy like taffy or caramels. Sorghum syrup is an excellent substitute for molasses when making gingerbread, spice cake, or barbecue sauce.

Molasses

Molasses is the syrup that's left over after boiling down sugar cane or sugar beets. Molasses is great to use when baking all types of cookies and cakes and for making candies. It is a must for spooning onto a piece of hot cornbread.

There are three basic types of molasses: dark (also known as cooking molasses), light (a milder molasses), and blackstrap (a very dark, thick molasses with a bitter flavor). Unsulfured molasses, which is what I recommend for cooking, does not contain any sulfur dioxide and is considered to be molasses in its purest form. All of these types of molasses can be found at most major grocery stores as well as natural food stores.

Brown Sugar

Brown sugar is sugar that gets its color from the addition of molasses, which probably explains why Southern cooks love to bake with it so much. Brown sugar can be purchased either as "light" or "dark," and there's not much difference between the two. While there's absolutely nothing wrong with plain, old white sugar, brown sugar is uniquely redolent with the flavor of burnt, caramelized sugar, making it hard to resist.

Cola, Dr. Pepper, and Ginger Ale

Sugary soda pop is a Southern cook's secret weapon. Not only does a cup or two of soda add a subtle sweetness and unique flavor; it also serves as both a marinade and a braising liquid when slow cooking meats like pork, ham, or chicken.

Savory Southern Seasonings

The key to cooking real-deal, down-home Southern food is incorporating the right ingredients. From ham hocks and bacon grease to tangy buttermilk and cider vinegar, here are some commonly used "seasonings" that will add Southern sass to your slow-cooked soups, stews, beans, breads, and desserts.

Bacon Grease (aka Bacon Fat, Drippings)

Often stored in a glass jar or "lard tin" can, these precious pork renderings can be used to flavor beans, potatoes, cabbage, gravies, biscuits, cornbread, and even apples and wilted lettuce salad. I'm a firm believer that fat renderings of any kind always taste best when cooked in cast iron.

Bacon

Side-meat bacon, which is the most popular type of bacon in the United States, is cured or smoked pork from the side belly of the pig. It's sold sliced and can have additional flavorings such as maple, applewood, or brown sugar.

Lard

Lard is what results from slow-cooking pork fat until the fat is melted and much of the water has been evaporated. It's often used to make biscuits and pie crusts and homemade soap. Also, it may come as a shock, but lard actually contains less saturated fat than butter.

Ham Hocks

Ham hocks are an inexpensive seasoning that comes from the ankle area of a pig's hind leg and can be purchased fresh, smoked, or cured. Hocks are best when added to slow-cooked beans (pinto beans, black-eyed peas, or lima beans) or greens such as collards, turnips, or kale.

Smoked Turkey Parts

Smoked turkey wings, legs, and necks lend a terrific flavor to greens, cabbage, beans and rice, navy bean soup, and even gumbo. They can be found in many grocery stores.

Vegetable Shortening

Vegetable shortening is similar to lard in that it's a solid fat, but instead of being rendered from animal fat, it's made from soybean oil. Vegetable shortening is great for frying chicken or fish since it has a high flash point, meaning it can withstand very high heat before smoking. It's also very popular for baking, particularly in pie crusts, cakes, and cookies.

Fatback

Fatback is a strip of uncured hard fat taken from the back of the pig. It is used to flavor pinto beans, collard greens, and black-eyed peas. Sometimes fatback is sold salted (as in salt pork). In that case, you need to wash or boil off the salt before cooking.

Buttermilk

Traditional buttermilk is the rich, tangy liquid that's left over from churning butter. However, what can be found in most grocery stores today is cultured buttermilk, which is fermented milk. Southerners use buttermilk in just about everything. Biscuits, fried chicken, pancakes, cobblers, mashed potatoes, even ice cream—these are just some of the many ways buttermilk is incorporated into our cooking.

Cider Vinegar

Apple cider vinegar is an amber-colored vinegar made from fermented apples; it's also a requirement for a well-stocked Southern kitchen. In addition to providing plenty of health benefits, cider vinegar gives many dishes, such as Carolina-style pulled pork barbecue, bread and butter pickles, and cole slaw, their unique tang. It's a must when cooking collard greens.

Black Walnuts

While the South is renowned for pecan anything and everything, black walnuts should not be overlooked. Black walnuts have a unique, strong, tannic flavor that is perfect when used in sweet cakes, pies, fudge, homemade candies, ice cream, and breads. Black walnuts can be purchased at most major grocery stores. If you're unable to find them, English walnuts can be substituted.

CHAPTER ONE

Soul-Warming
Soups, Stews, and Chilis

The Big Black Pot

Simmering soups, stews, and chilis made with end-of-the-summer vegetables and a piece of meat or fat is a Southern tradition born out of necessity. With the arrival of fall, what remained of summer's bounty that was not "put up" (canned) made its way into the cast-iron kettle where it boiled away for hours, often over a hot fire. Delicacies like slow-cooked "shelley" beans (aka limas or butter beans), vegetable soup, potato soup, and corn soup could feed a large family for days, and what wasn't eaten could be frozen or canned for later.

Many familiar soups and stews such as Brunswick, gumbo, and Kentucky burgoo originated from this style of cooking, with the outdoor iron kettle eventually being replaced by traditional stovetop cooking pots and Dutch ovens. These were recipes that were hearty enough to require nothing more than a wedge of cornbread to round out the meal. While most of these one-pot wonders were simply flavored with just meat, water, salt, and pepper, many cooks placed their own particular spins on their dishes

Take chicken and dumplings, for example. While many cooks make this rich, satisfying stew with biscuit-type dumplings dropped into the chicken broth mixture, others insist that it can only be cooked with rolled pastry that's cut into squares and then added into the stew. Even the name is highly debated; some call it chicken and dumplings and others call it chicken and pastry. It all depends on where you're from and how your mom or grandma taught you to make it. In this chapter, I've included a slow-cooker chicken and dumplings (page 32) that doesn't subscribe to either one of these cooking schools of thought. It features fluffy cornmeal dumplings resting in a much lighter-style broth than is typical of this classic Southern dish. What results are airy, crumbly dumplings in a savory broth that's more like a soup than a stew.

Chili is another hearty one-pot meal the preparation and ingredients of which is often debated with passion. Beans or no beans, ground beef or cubed chuck roast, tomatoes or none are just a few of the many variations out there that cooks (especially chili experts) can feel very strongly about. I've decided to stir the chili debate pot a bit more and have included a couple of slow-cooker recipes including one using ground buffalo meat, beans, a wee bit of tomato sauce, and bottle of dark beer (page 31). I also just had to include a classic Frito pie (page 35), which takes a traditional ground beef-type chili and adds Fritos corn chips, grated cheddar, sour cream, and onions. Comfort food doesn't get much better than this, and the best part is that this recipe, like others in this chapter, is designed to be cooked in the slow cooker, so you can come home from work to the enticing aroma of spices, meat, and beans with dinner on the table in no time.

Mom's Fully Loaded Potato and Onion Soup

We call this family recipe for creamy potato soup "fully loaded," not only because it's chock full of potatoes, onions, celery, butter, and cream, but because you can add even more decadence by topping it with crispy fried bacon bits, grated cheddar cheese, and green onions. A little goes a long way for this indulgent soup, so all you need to make it a meal is a fresh green salad.

Serves 4 to 6

4 large baking or russet potatoes,
   cut into 1½-inch cubes (4 to 5 cups)
½ cup chopped celery
1 cup coarsely chopped onion
About 4 cups water
1 teaspoon salt, plus more as needed
3 tablespoons all-purpose flour
1 cup whole milk, chilled
1 cup half-and-half
2 tablespoons unsalted butter
2 teaspoons granulated chicken
   bouillon
1 teaspoon dried parsley
1 teaspoon dried thyme
Pinch of cayenne (optional)
Salt and black pepper

TOPPINGS
Cooked, crumbled bacon pieces
Grated sharp cheddar cheese
Minced green onions
   (white and green parts)

Spray the inside of your slow cooker with cooking spray. Layer the potatoes, celery, and onions in the slow cooker. Add the water to just cover the vegetables and stir in the salt. Cover and cook on low for 6 to 7 hours, until the potatoes are fork-tender and the vegetable have softened.

In a microwave-safe bowl, whisk the flour into the milk, dissolving any lumps. Add the half-and-half, butter, and granulated chicken bouillon. Cover and cook in the microwave on high for 15 to 20 seconds, just until it starts to simmer. Add this mixture to the slow cooker and give it a stir. Add the parsley, thyme, and cayenne. Cover and cook on low for another 50 to 60 minutes. Mash about half of the potatoes with a potato masher or with a fork. Season generously with salt and pepper, the more black pepper the better.

Spoon into bowls. Pass the toppings at the table to enjoy the soup "fully loaded."

Note: For an extra-cheesy, thicker soup, mix 1 cup grated cheddar cheese into the soup and cook for an additional 30 minutes.

TO DRINK   A tropical, floral Viognier, such as Virginia's Blenheim Vineyards 2011 Viognier

Smoked Ham, Potato, and Rice Soup

This hearty soup is ideal for serving a crowd and costs little to make, so it's great for the budget-conscious cook. Smoky ham, diced potatoes, and long-grain rice are simmered in a rich chicken broth accented with plenty of herbs, a bit of butter, and just a swirl of tomato paste to give it depth and color. This soup is an excellent way to use up any leftover ham from the Dr. Pepper Sorghum Roasted Ham (page 54), so be sure to save all those little pieces of meat and toss in the leftover hambone for extra flavor. The soup is a meal in itself, so I recommend serving it with a simple green salad and a wedge of classic Southern cornbread (page 124) or thick slices of multigrain bread.

Serves 10

3 cups sliced onions

1 pound smoked ham, diced

3 cloves garlic, minced

3 cups peeled and diced baking or russet potatoes

¼ cup unsalted butter, cut into pieces

¼ cup tomato paste

8 cups chicken broth, low sodium or homemade (page 122)

2 bay leaves

½ teaspoon dried parsley

¼ teaspoon dried savory

¼ teaspoon dried thyme

¼ cup uncooked long-grain rice

Salt and black pepper

Spray a large slow cooker with cooking spray and add the onions, ham, garlic, potatoes, butter, tomato paste, chicken broth, bay leaves, parsley, savory, and thyme. Stir together, cover, and cook on low for 8 hours.

Stir in the rice and cook for another 15 minutes, or until the rice is tender; watch it very closely so you don't overcook it. Remove the bay leaves, then season with salt and pepper and serve.

TO DRINK   A rich, fruity hard cider, such as Virginia's Foggy Ridge First Fruit cider

Zesty Beef and Cabbage Soup

This comforting blend of ground beef, cabbage, beans, and spiced tomatoes is almost as much a stew as it is a soup. Hearty, nourishing, and fit for a chilly day, this is a recipe that's easy to whip up in a pinch since you may have some of the ingredients already on hand.

Serves 8 to 10

1 tablespoon vegetable oil
12 ounces lean ground beef
2 cups diced onions
3 cups chopped cabbage
¾ cup diced celery
2 (14.5-ounce) cans diced tomatoes with juice
1 (10-ounce) can diced tomatoes with green chiles (such as Rotel brand) with its juice
1 (14.5-ounce) can red kidney beans, rinsed and drained
1 (14.5-ounce) can whole kernel corn, drained
1 (14.5-ounce) can baby lima beans, rinsed and drained
1 (8-ounce) can Italian herb-flavored tomato sauce or regular tomato sauce
5 cups chicken broth, low sodium or homemade (page 122)
3 beef bouillon cubes
1 tablespoon Worcestershire sauce
1 teaspoon prepared horseradish
2 tablespoons dried parsley
⅛ teaspoon cayenne pepper (optional)
1 teaspoon sugar (optional)
Salt and black pepper
Salty crackers, to serve

Heat a large skillet or cast-iron pan on the stovetop over medium-high heat. Add the oil. Crumble in the beef, add the onions, and cook until the beef is browned, about 5 minutes. Drain on paper towels.

Spray the inside of the slow cooker with cooking spray. Add the beef to the slow cooker along with the cabbage, celery, both types of canned tomatoes, kidney beans, corn, lima beans, tomato sauce, chicken broth, bouillon cubes, Worcestershire sauce, and horseradish. Cover and cook on low for at least 6 hours and up to 8 hours.

During the last hour of cooking, add the parsley, cayenne, and sugar. Season with salt and pepper.

Spoon into bowls and serve with salty crackers.

Smoky Navy Bean Soup

Few meals are heartier than a bowl of slow-cooked, tender beans, and this recipe sure fits the bill. Smoked turkey parts (wings, backs, and necks) are a great way to season all types of dishes, from collard greens to Hoppin' John. If you can't get your hands on smoked turkey wings, a smoked ham hock, pork neck, leftover ham bone, or 12 ounces of cooked, diced, smoked bacon works equally well. • This recipe is ideal for overnight cooking. Once, after cooking it for 11 hours on low, I left it in my slow cooker on the "warm" setting for an additional 6 hours. Even after 17 hours in the slow cooker, it still tasted outstanding.

Serves 10 to 12

1 pound dried navy beans

1 large smoked turkey wing, about 12 ounces

1 cup chopped onion

1 cup finely diced carrots

½ cup diced celery

2 cloves garlic, minced

1 bay leaf

1 teaspoon dried thyme

About 4 cups chicken broth, low sodium or homemade (page 122)

Water (optional)

Salt and black pepper

Pinch of dried cayenne pepper (optional)

Cornbread (page 124), to serve

Rinse and pick through the beans, discarding any debris. Put them in a large bowl, cover with water by at least 2 inches, and soak overnight. Rinse and drain.

Spray the slow cooker with cooking spray. Add the beans, turkey wing, onion, carrot, celery, garlic, bay leaf, and thyme. Pour in the chicken broth—it should cover the beans by at least ½ inch. Cover and cook on low for 10 to 12 hours, until the beans are tender, adding additional water to the pot if necessary to cover the beans.

Remove the turkey wing and let cool. Discard the bay leaf.

Shred the meat off the turkey bone and discard the bones and skin. Return the turkey meat to the pot. Season with salt and pepper (I recommend being generous with black pepper) and cayenne. Serve with wedges of cornbread.

Manhattan Clam Chowder

I have to admit, this recipe's title is about the only truly Southern thing it has going for it. Either way, I just had to include it since this recipe is as soul satisfying as any down-home country-style chowder I've ever had. Even better, this chowder works great in the slow cooker and makes plenty to feed a crowd when entertaining. Serve this hearty soup with a slice of rustic sourdough bread and a side salad for an easy weeknight meal.

Serves 8 to 10

6 strips bacon
1 cup boiling water
2 beef bouillon cubes
1 cup diced onion
1 cup diced carrots
¼ cup diced celery
5 cups diced and peeled baking or
   russet potatoes (½-inch pieces)
3 cups Clamato juice
1 (14.5-ounce) can diced tomatoes
   and juice
1 (10-ounce) can diced tomatoes
   with mild green chiles (such as Rotel
   brand) with its juice
1¼ cups chicken broth, low sodium
   or homemade (page 122)
1 tablespoon Worcestershire sauce
1 tablespoon dried parsley
¼ teaspoon dried thyme
2 bay leaves
1 teaspoon black pepper
⅛ teaspoon cayenne pepper (optional)
4 (6.5-ounce) cans minced clams
   with their juice
Salt
Minced fresh parsley, for serving

Spray a 6-quart or larger slow cooker with cooking spray.

Heat a large sauté pan or cast-iron skillet on the stovetop over medium-high heat, add the bacon, and cook until crisp, about 10 to 12 minutes. Drain on paper towels, crumble, and set aside.

In a small saucepan on the stovetop, dissolve the bouillon cubes in the water. Combine the onion, carrots, celery, potatoes, Clamato juice, both types of tomatoes, chicken broth, Worcestershire sauce, parsley, thyme, bay leaves, black pepper, and cayenne in the slow cooker. Add the bacon, the bouillon mixture, and the clams and their juice. Stir, cover, and cook on low for at least 8 hours and up to 10 hours.

Remove the bay leaves and add salt to taste. To serve, ladle the chowder into bowls and sprinkle with parsley.

TO DRINK   A medium-bodied, fruity red wine, such as North Carolina's Hanover Park Winery Chambourcin

Blue Crab and Corn Chowder
WITH SWEET CORN RELISH

Blue crabs from the Chesapeake Bay offer a delectable sweet meat unlike any other. From April through November, blue crabs are in season, and they get bigger and meatier as the months go by. As a result, blue crabs tend to peak later in the summer. While this recipe calls for frozen corn kernels, you should feel free to substitute fresh corn—just be sure to add it at the same time you add the crab, so the corn doesn't overcook. • For extra flair, serve soup from a bread bowl made from hollowed-out mini boules. Freeze the hollowed-out bread pieces for making homemade bread crumbs later. Making the corn relish is optional but highly recommended.

Serves 6 to 8

4 cups chicken broth, low sodium or homemade (page 122)

3 cups frozen corn kernels

2 cups peeled and diced baking or russet potatoes

1 large onion, diced

¼ cup celery, diced

2 tablespoons unsalted butter

1 tablespoon dried parsley

2 teaspoon garlic, minced

1 teaspoon Worcestershire sauce

½ teaspoon prepared horseradish

¼ teaspoon dried thyme

¼ teaspoon ground nutmeg

Pinch of cayenne pepper (optional)

1 bay leaf

1 cup heavy cream

1 tablespoon cooking sherry

1 pound fresh crabmeat, picked through

1 tablespoon all-purpose flour mixed to a paste with 1 tablespoon softened unsalted butter

Salt and black pepper

Old Bay Seasoning

Sweet Corn Relish (recipe follows)

Fresh minced chives, for garnish

Extra virgin olive oil, to serve (optional)

Spray the slow cooker with cooking spray. Add the chicken broth, corn, potatoes, onion, celery, butter, parsley, garlic, Worcestershire sauce, horseradish, thyme, nutmeg, cayenne, and bay leaf. Stir to combine; then cover and cook on low for at least 7 hours and up to 8 hours.

Add the heavy cream, sherry, and crabmeat. Whisk in the flour and butter paste. Cover and cook on high for another 1½ to 2 hours. Uncover the pot during the last 30 to 45 minutes to allow the soup to thicken a bit, stirring it occasionally. Season with salt, black pepper, and Old Bay to taste. Remove the bay leaf.

Ladle the chowder into bowls and top with a generous dollop of the corn relish and a sprinkling of chives. Drizzle the soup with some quality olive oil for a special presentation.

TO DRINK   An un-oaked Chardonnay, such as Virginia's Prince Michel Winery Rapidan River Chardonnay

continued

Blue Crab and Corn Chowder, continued

Sweet Corn Relish

This fresh-from-the-garden combination makes an excellent dip for corn chips or a bruschetta topping, so hold onto any leftovers. If you don't have fresh corn, you can substitute canned, drained corn or frozen corn that has been blanched and drained. *Makes 3 cups*

2 cups fresh corn kernels (from about 3 ears)
2½ tablespoons cider vinegar
1½ teaspoons sugar
1 teaspoon extra virgin olive oil
¼ teaspoon salt
¼ teaspoon celery seeds
⅛ teaspoon black pepper
¼ cup diced red bell pepper
¼ cup diced green bell pepper
¼ cup peeled, seeded, and diced cucumber
¼ cup diced red onion
1 small tomato, seeded and diced

Bring a pot of salted water to a gentle boil. Add the corn and simmer for 1 minute. Drain and set aside.

In a bowl, mix together the vinegar, sugar, olive oil, salt, celery seeds, and black pepper until the sugar has completely dissolved. Add the red bell pepper, green bell pepper, cucumber, red onion, tomato, and corn and mix well. Cover and store in the refrigerator for at least 1 hour and up to 3 days.

Buffalo Stout Beer Chili

Ground buffalo meat is ground beef's leaner, healthier cousin—and it makes a flavor-packed chili in the slow cooker. This recipe gets an extra kick from the addition of dark beer, preferably an Irish stout (such as Guinness or Murphy's) or a milk stout (such as Left Hand), which adds a hint of smokiness and coffee-like flavor to this heavily spiced chili.

Serves 8 to 10

2 pounds ground buffalo meat
1 large onion, diced
3 cloves garlic, minced
1 (8-ounce) can tomato sauce
1 (10-ounce) can diced tomatoes with
   green chiles, such as Rotel brand
1 teaspoon Worcestershire sauce
3 tablespoons chili powder
1 teaspoon cumin
1 teaspoon dried oregano
1 teaspoon brown sugar
½ teaspoon ground cinnamon
½ teaspoon ground allspice
¼ teaspoon cayenne pepper (optional)
1 bay leaf
1 (12-ounce) bottle dark beer,
   preferably a stout
6 tablespoons tomato paste (3 ounces)
2 (15-ounce) cans pinto beans,
   drained and rinsed
Salt and black pepper

OPTIONAL THICKENER
2 tablespoons fine corn flour
2 tablespoons cold water

OPTIONAL GARNISHES
Cheddar cheese, grated
Green onions, both green and white
   parts, minced
Fresh cilantro, chopped
Sour cream
Hot sauce
Tortilla chips or cornbread (page 124)

Spray the inside of large slow cooker with cooking spray.

Heat a large saucepan on the stovetop over medium-high heat. Crumble in the buffalo meat and cook until well browned, about 7 to 8 minutes. Use a slotted spoon to transfer the meat to the slow cooker. Drain off half the fat in the saucepan and discard it. Add the onion and garlic to the remaining fat and sauté until translucent, 6 to 8 minutes.

Pour the onion, garlic, and pan juices into the slow cooker. Add the tomato sauce, tomatoes, Worcestershire sauce, chili powder, cumin, oregano, brown sugar, cinnamon, allspice, cayenne, bay leaf, beer, and tomato paste. Give it a stir and add the pinto beans. Cover and cook on low for at least 8 hours and up to 10 hours, skimming off any surface fat from time to time.

If you prefer a thicker chili, during the last 45 to 60 minutes before serving, mix together the fine corn flour and cold water in a small bowl. Then, remove the lid, crank the slow cooker up to high, and whisk in the corn flour mixture.

During the last 15 minutes of cooking, season with salt and pepper.

Remove the bay leaf. Serve the chili topped with the garnishes or pass them on the side.

TO DRINK A cold glass of Duck-Rabbit Milk Stout from North Carolina or similar rich, dark stout beer

Chicken and Cornmeal Dumplings

This hearty, flavorful recipe is not as simple as the traditional creamy chicken and dumplings, but it's worth the extra effort. Instead of swirling flour-based dumplings (like thick-cut noodles) into a stew, this version has you dropping in rounded dumplings made from a mixture of fine cornmeal and buttermilk. The result is a brothier, gently seasoned soup with puffy dumplings and lots of chicken. It is lightly thickened by incorporating a *beurre manié* (a paste made from equal parts butter and flour). Also, since this recipe has a long cooking time (around 12 hours from start to finish), be sure to get your chicken in the pot early in the morning in order to have your soup be finished and on the table by dinner time. • Alternatively, you can get a head start by slow-cooking the chicken the day before. If you do cook the chicken in advance, strain the broth into a bowl and then store the broth and cooked chicken separately in the fridge until you are ready to use it. Scrape the fat layer (which will be clearly visible) off the chilled broth before returning it to the pot. Proceed with the rest of the recipe.

Serves 8

1 large onion, sliced

2 large carrots, cut into chunks

2 celery stalks, cut into chunks

2 cloves garlic, smashed

1 bay leaf

1 (4- to 5-pound) chicken

¼ teaspoon black pepper,
 plus more to taste

2 cups chicken broth, low sodium
 or homemade (page 122)

4 cups water

½ cup whole milk

1 tablespoon all-purpose flour

1 teaspoon dried parsley

1 teaspoon dried thyme

2 tablespoons all-purpose flour mixed
 with 2 tablespoons softened
 unsalted butter to a paste

Salt and black pepper

Spray the inside of the slow cooker with cooking spray. Layer the onion, carrots, celery, garlic, and bay leaf in the slow cooker. Add the chicken, breast side up, and sprinkle it with black pepper. Pour in the chicken broth and water. Cover and cook on low for 8 to 10 hours, until the chicken is fall-off-the-bone tender.

Transfer the chicken to a large bowl and let cool. Meanwhile, strain the cooking liquid through a fine sieve or colander, pressing out the solids (discard the vegetables). Skim the fat off with a ladle and discard. Alternatively, you can refrigerate the broth for 30 minutes or until the fat rises to the top and solidifies before removing it. Remove the skin and bones from the chicken and shred the meat. (Save the skin and bones for making stock later if you like.)

Return the strained broth to the slow cooker and add the chicken; cover and turn the heat up to high. Meanwhile, mix the milk and flour together in a small bowl. When the broth begins to simmer, stir in the milk and flour mixture and the parsley and thyme. Season generously to taste with salt and pepper. Finally, drop the flour and butter mix into the broth in pieces and whisk in. Cover and bring to a simmer.

DUMPLINGS

1 cup all-purpose flour
¼ cup fine yellow cornmeal
2 teaspoons baking powder
¼ teaspoon salt
2 tablespoons vegetable shortening
1 egg, beaten
½ cup buttermilk
Minced fresh chives, for garnish
     (optional)

Meanwhile, make the dumplings. In a large bowl, mix together flour, cornmeal, baking powder, and salt. Using two knives or a pastry cutter, cut in the shortening until crumbly. Stir in the egg and the buttermilk with a fork. Wet your hands with water and gently roll the cornmeal mixture into 1-inch balls.

When the chicken broth mixture is simmering, drop the dumplings on top of the chicken mixture. If they sink, don't worry; they'll float back to the top. Cover and cook for 45 to 60 minutes or until a toothpick inserted into a dumpling comes out clean. (Resist the urge to lift the lid during those first 45 minutes of cooking time; otherwise, the dumplings will have trouble cooking through.)

Remove the bay leaf. Spoon the chicken soup and dumplings into bowls and garnish with the chives and extra black pepper. Break up the dumplings as you eat them so they soak up all that delicious broth.

Note: This soup doesn't really keep well; if you store any leftovers in the fridge, the dumplings will start to dissolve into the broth.

Frito Pie with Chili con Carne

It's hard to go wrong when you combine homemade chili, onions, and cheddar cheese with addictively crunchy Fritos corn chips, and you can serve this decadent treat with your chips piled high in a big bowl topped with warm chili and all the fixin's, or "walking taco" style, with the chili dumped right into an individual serving–size bag of Fritos. However you decide to dive into this Southwestern-style treat, one thing's for certain: this is one tasty combination with a highly debated origin. One theory argues that the first Frito pie was created by Frito-Lay founder Elmer Doolin's mother in Texas, but New Mexico also stakes claim to the first Frito and bean combo as originating from a lunch counter in Santa Fe. Either way, this indulgent recipe satisfies the kid in all of us and is made for potlucks, family reunions, and tailgating.

Serves 8

1 teaspoon bacon grease or vegetable oil

2 pounds extra-lean ground beef

4 cloves garlic, minced

3 tablespoons chili powder

1½ teaspoons cumin

1 teaspoon dried oregano, preferably Mexican

¾ teaspoon salt

½ teaspoon sugar

¼ teaspoon black pepper

¼ teaspoon cayenne pepper (optional)

2 (8-ounce) cans tomato sauce

1 (10-ounce) can diced tomatoes with green chiles (such as Rotel brand) with its juice

2 (14-ounce) cans kidney beans, rinsed and drained

FOR SERVING

8 ounces sharp cheddar cheese, grated

½ cup minced sweet onion

Sliced pickled jalapeños

Sour cream

Large (14-ounce) bag Fritos brand corn chips, or 8 (1- or 2-ounce) individual serving–size bags

Spray the inside of the slow cooker with cooking spray.

Heat a large skillet or cast-iron pan on the stovetop over medium-high heat and add the bacon grease. Crumble in the ground beef and cook until the meat is no longer pink, about 5 minutes. Add the garlic and cook for another minute. Mix in the chili powder, cumin, oregano, salt, sugar, black pepper, and cayenne. Cook for 1 more minute.

Pour the beef mixture into the slow cooker and add the tomato sauce, tomatoes and chiles, and kidney beans. Stir well. Cover and cook on low for at least 8 hours and up to 9 hours.

To serve, spread the chips in a 9 by 13-inch casserole dish or divide among eight smaller bowls. Pour in the chili, then top with the cheddar, sweet onion, jalapeños, and sour cream and serve. Alternatively, cut open eight individual serving–size bags of chips, divide the chili and toppings evenly among the bags, and eat straight from the bags with a fork.

TO DRINK An icy-cold Lone Star lager from Texas or similar light brew

Aunt Barbara's Beef Stew

The grand-daddy of all heart-warming dishes, this recipe was passed on to me by my Aunt Barbara in Fairmont, West Virginia, where it can get awfully cold outside. I figure this dish did wonders to warm both her kitchen and her soul on many occasions. This classic beef stew recipe contains all the familiar elements: stew meat, onions, potato, carrots, and lots of herbs and spices, even a sprig of fresh rosemary, if you like. Serve with biscuits (page 123), cornbread (page 124), or a chunk of hearty bread for the ultimate comfort food meal.

Serves 6 to 8

2½ cups coarsely chopped onions

4 carrots, peeled and cut into 1½-inch slices

2 large baking or russet potatoes, peeled and cut into 1½-inch cubes (about 2½ cups)

1½ pounds boneless beef stew meat, trimmed of any visible excess fat and cut into 1-inch pieces

½ cup all-purpose flour

½ teaspoon salt

¼ teaspoon black pepper

1 tablespoon bacon grease, vegetable oil, or unsalted butter

½ cup red wine

3 cups beef broth, low sodium or homemade

1 (15-ounce) can diced tomatoes with its juice

2 tablespoons tomato paste

1 tablespoon Worcestershire sauce

3 cloves garlic, minced

2 bay leaves

½ teaspoon sugar

½ teaspoon dried parsley

¼ teaspoon paprika

¼ teaspoon dried oregano

¼ teaspoon dried thyme

¼ teaspoon dried basil

Sprig of fresh rosemary (optional)

Salt and black pepper

Chopped fresh rosemary or parsley, to garnish (optional)

Spray the inside of the slow cooker with cooking spray. Layer the onions, carrots, and potatoes in the slow cooker.

Combine the stew meat, flour, salt, and black pepper in a large resealable plastic bag and shake to coat well. Heat a large cast-iron skillet or nonstick pan over medium-high heat. Add the bacon grease and let it melt. Shake the excess flour off the stew meat and add enough to fill the pan without crowding (you may have to do this in batches). Brown well on all sides, about 5 minutes, then transfer the meat to the slow cooker.

Add the wine to the skillet and cook for 1 minute. Add the beef broth. Using a wooden spoon, scrape up all the bits off the bottom of the pan and immediately transfer the stew meat and broth mixture to the slow cooker.

Add the tomatoes, tomato paste, Worcestershire sauce, garlic, bay leaves, sugar, parsley, paprika, oregano, thyme, and basil. Give it a stir. Toss in the rosemary. Cover and cook on low for 8 to 10 hours, until the meat is tender and the stew has thickened.

Uncover, discard the bay leaves and the rosemary sprig, and season with salt and pepper. At this point, if you desire an even thicker stew, you can crank up the heat to high and continue to cook, uncovered, until thickened.

Serve the stew in bowls garnished with additional rosemary or fresh parsley, if desired.

CHAPTER TWO

Low and Slow Meats

Turn It to Low and Cook It Slow

I can think of no better function for the slow cooker than for cooking beef, pork, or chicken. Steady, low and slow heat over many hours does wonders for tough cuts of beef or pork, and it can tenderize a whole chicken until it is falling off the bone. Slow cooking breaks down the tough collagen while still preserving the moisture in the meat.

Preparing meals in the slow cooker allows the home cook to easily create dishes using various cuts of beef, pork, or chicken that cost significantly less per pound than their quick-grilling counterparts. Most likely, there will be plenty of leftovers for lunch the next day. Slow cooking tough cuts of meat takes time, often lots of it, so many of the recipes in this chapter are ideal for overnight cooking or while you're at work.

Meats, such as filet mignon, cooked quickly at very high temperatures are certainly part of the Southern repertoire, but what we truly embrace are those highly flavored cuts of pork that cook for hours until they break down into a pile of tender, meaty bliss. Behold the Southern barbecue.

Southern barbecue (also known as barbeque, BBQ, or bar-b-q) is an honest-to-goodness, south of the Mason-Dixon Line creation, with a rich history that's traceable back to before the Civil War. During this time, pork was a Southern staple because semi-wild pigs were far more abundant than farm-raised beef. As a result, the diet of the average Southerner was quite pig heavy, and every part of the animal was put to good use, especially the tougher cuts of meat. Picnic shoulders, Boston butt roasts, and spareribs were slathered with a vinegar-based or sweet tomato-based sauce while they cooked over a low fire for hours upon hours, until the richly flavored meat fell from the bone.

Southern barbecue has stood the test of time and is today more popular than ever. Its culinary stylings are still hotly contested—vinegar sauce versus mustard, pulled pork versus chopped; even what toppings should grace your sandwich can start a dispute. Southerners might feel strongly about their slow-cooked pork, and you'll find plenty of pork recipes here, but one thing remains a constant: Whether it's for beef brisket, barbecued chicken, sausages, or ham, all of these recipes taste best after bubbling away for hours.

So sit back, put your feet up, and let the slow cooker do all the work.

Beer-Braised Beef Po' Boys

The po' boy sandwich is a true New Orleans original, and the story goes that the first one was created by two restaurant owners, Benny and Clovis Martin, who were former streetcar drivers. During the 1920s, the Martin brothers stuffed French bread rolls with inexpensive bits of roast beef and gravy. When their fellow streetcar drivers went on strike in 1929, the Martins decided to offer them free sandwiches. When a displaced driver entered the restaurant to partake of this generosity, the kitchen would announce, "Here comes another po' boy!" and thus the po' boy sandwich was born. Po' boys can be filled with just about anything, from fried oysters and catfish to a simple combination of ham and cheese, but one thing always remains the same—every po' boy must be properly "dressed" with shredded lettuce, tomatoes, dill pickles, and mayonnaise. • This recipe is all about roast beef, which is a classic po' boy filler. Beef chuck roast is slow-cooked all day in a savory broth made with garlic, herbs, and beer until it's divinely shreddable and the perfect sandwich filler. When it comes to beer, just about any richly flavored dark beer will work, but it's the brown, malty Belgian Abbey Dubbels that make this dish really shine. Save leftover cooking liquid (the *jus*) from the cooked roast to serve as a dipping sauce for the sandwiches.

Serves 8

1½ cups sliced onion

1 (3-pound) beef chuck roast, trimmed of excess fat

4 cloves garlic, coarsely chopped

½ teaspoon salt, plus more as needed

½ teaspoon black pepper, plus more as needed

½ teaspoon paprika

½ teaspoon onion powder

½ teaspoon dried thyme

¼ teaspoon dried oregano

⅛ teaspoon cayenne pepper

2 cups beef broth, low sodium or homemade

1 cup light to amber-colored Belgian-style Abbey Ale (such as Chimay) or any dark beer

TO SERVE

8 soft sub rolls or French bread cut into 8-inch lengths

Mayonnaise

Shredded lettuce

Sliced tomatoes

Sliced dill pickles

Spray the inside of the slow cooker with cooking spray. Put the onion in the slow cooker.

Cut small slits into the beef and stud with pieces of garlic. In a small bowl, mix together the salt, black pepper, paprika, onion powder, thyme, oregano, and cayenne. Rub this into the meat and place the meat in the slow cooker on top of the onions. Pour the beef broth and beer over the meat. Cover and cook on low for at least 8 hours or up to 10 hours, until the meat is easily shredded.

Transfer the meat and onions to a large bowl and shred the meat with two forks. Remove 2¼ cups of the cooking liquid from the slow cooker and pour that over the shredded beef. Pour any remaining broth left in the slow cooker into a bowl for *jus*. Return the meat and broth mixture to the slow cooker and set it on warm. Season with additional salt and pepper and give it a stir.

To serve, slather the inside of the rolls with mayonnaise. Add the shredded beef and top with shredded lettuce, tomatoes, and pickles. Serve the *jus* in a bowl for dipping. Get out a big pile of napkins and enjoy.

TO DRINK   A Belgian Dubbel, such as Abita Abbey Ale from Louisiana

Rustic Pot Roast with Bacon, Garlic, and Rosemary

This saucy pot roast simply bursts with aromatics like garlic, rosemary and onions, but arguably it's the bacon, with its hint of smokiness, that makes this dish truly divine. Also, since this recipe has potatoes in it, no complicated sides are required. Just serve your pot roast with a green salad and crusty bread. For this recipe, I definitely recommend using a 5-quart or larger slow cooker depending on the size of your roast.

Serves 6 to 8

2 slices of bacon, diced

3- to 4-pound boneless chuck roast, trimmed of excess fat

Salt and black pepper

1½ teaspoons olive oil

1 cup beef broth, low sodium or homemade

2 onions, chopped

1 stalk celery, chopped

2 russet or baking potatoes, peeled and chopped

5 cloves garlic, smashed

1 (14-ounce) can diced tomatoes with its juice

1 tablespoon tomato paste

2 sprigs rosemary, plus more to garnish

Spray the inside of the slow cooker with cooking spray.

Heat a large Dutch oven or cast-iron pan on the stovetop over medium-high heat. Add the bacon and cook until crispy, about 5 minutes. Drain on paper towels. Pour off all but 1 teaspoon of the bacon drippings.

Sprinkle the beef with salt and pepper on all sides (go easy on the salt if using canned beef stock, which is already salty). Add the olive oil to the pan with the drippings, then, over medium-high heat, brown the beef well on all sides, about 6-8 minutes. Transfer the meat to the slow cooker and then, over medium-high heat, deglaze the pan with beef broth, scraping up all the bits on the bottom of the pan. Pour the juices from the pan into the slow cooker.

Add the onions, celery, potatoes, garlic, tomatoes, tomato paste, and rosemary to the slow cooker. Finally add the bacon. Stir everything well, nestling the vegetables and rosemary into the broth. Cover and cook on low for at least 7 hours and up to 8 hours, until the meat is very tender.

Transfer the meat to a platter and turn the slow cooker to high. Leave the slow cooker uncovered and continue cooking the sauce for 45 minutes, or until it has thickened some. Return the meat to the slow cooker and continue to cook uncovered on high for another 15 to 30 minutes, or until the sauce has thickened a bit more.

Remove the rosemary sprigs and discard. Season the sauce with additional salt and pepper, if needed. Plate the beef on a large platter and spoon the potatoes and sauce around and over the beef. Garnish with additional rosemary sprigs. Save any extra sauce for bread dipping.

TO DRINK   A Nebbiolo, such as one from Barboursville Vineyards in Virginia

Porcupine Meatballs

This hearty, slow-cooked, tomato-based dish gets its name from the long-grain rice that is blended into the meatball mixture giving it a quill-like quality. This is comfort food at its finest and an ideal cold-weather meal. Serve these delicate meatballs topped with grated Parmesan alongside a green salad and a wedge of crusty bread for soaking up any leftover sauce. For an amazing second-day meal, you can make meatball subs: just spoon some warm meatballs into sub rolls, top with provolone cheese, and broil until the cheese melts. • The meatballs are different from traditional Italian meatballs. They are more fragile, so avoid stirring them too much, or they'll fall apart. If they do break apart, no worries, just serve them over mashed potatoes, which is another great combination.

Serves 6

SAUCE

1 (28-ounce) can diced tomatoes, drained
1 (10-ounce) can diced tomatoes with green chiles (such as Rotel brand), drained
1 (5.5-ounce) can tomato juice
1 (10.75-ounce) can tomato soup
1 cup water
2 teaspoons Worcestershire sauce
1½ teaspoons sugar
1 teaspoon dried oregano
1 teaspoon dried parsley
2 bay leaves

Spray the inside of the slow cooker with cooking spray.

To make the sauce, add both cans of tomatoes, the tomato juice, tomato soup, water, Worcestershire sauce, sugar, oregano, dried parsley, and bay leaves to the slow cooker and stir well.

ingredients and method continued

MEATBALLS

1½ pounds extra-lean ground beef

½ cup uncooked long-grain rice

1 small onion, diced

½ cup milk

1 egg, beaten

1 tablespoon Worcestershire sauce

1½ teaspoons prepared horseradish

2 cloves garlic, minced

1 teaspoon dried basil

1 teaspoon dried oregano

½ teaspoon salt

¼ teaspoon black pepper

Pinch of celery salt

2 tablespoons olive oil

Salt and black pepper

Fresh flat-leaf parsley, minced,
    for garnish

Grated Parmesan cheese, for garnish

To make the meatballs, mix together the beef, rice, onion, milk, egg, Worcestershire sauce, horseradish, garlic, basil, oregano, salt, pepper, and celery salt in a large bowl. Gently form into round balls 1½ to 2 inches in diameter.

Heat a large sauté pan on the stovetop over medium-high heat. Add the olive oil. Add the meatballs and brown well on all sides, about 5 to 7 minutes.

When the meatballs are all browned, add them to the slow cooker along with the pan juices. Stir gently once or twice until all of the meatballs are coated in sauce, being careful not to break them up. Cover and cook on low at least 6 hours, and up to 8 hours.

If you would prefer a thicker sauce, set the slow cooker to high and uncover it for the last 30 to 45 minutes of cooking, or until the sauce is thickened. Season with salt and pepper. Remove the bay leaves.

To serve, spoon the meatballs and sauce into individual serving bowls and top with fresh parsley and Parmesan cheese.

Meatloaf with Brown Sugar BBQ Sauce

Sometimes there's nothing more comforting than a plate of meatloaf and mashed potatoes. This meatloaf recipe doesn't go the standard gravy route; instead, a piquant barbecue sauce is added to the meat mixture, then slathered on top during the last bit of cooking. What results is a tangy, tender meatloaf with a moist, steamy quality. Cooking the meatloaf in tin foil inserted into the slow cooker not only makes for easy clean-up, but the entire loaf can be lifted right out of the insert for easy serving.

Serves 6

SAUCE

1½ cups ketchup
2 small garlic cloves, minced
¼ cup firmly packed brown sugar
1 tablespoon apple cider vinegar
2 teaspoons Worcestershire sauce
1 teaspoon chili powder
1 teaspoon hot sauce (optional)
½ teaspoon soy sauce
Salt and black pepper

MEATLOAF

2 eggs
3 tablespoons finely minced or
   grated onion
1½ pounds extra-lean ground beef
   (or a mix of ground pork and beef)
1½ cups old-fashioned rolled oats
½ cup buttermilk
1½ teaspoons Worcestershire sauce
½ teaspoon prepared horseradish
1 teaspoon salt
½ teaspoon black pepper

To make the sauce, combine the ketchup, garlic, brown sugar, cider vinegar, Worcestershire sauce, chili powder, hot sauce, and soy sauce in a saucepan on the stovetop. Simmer over medium-low heat for 15 to 20 minutes until the sugar has dissolved and the sauce is slightly thickened. Season with salt and pepper and set aside. Let cool and set aside 3 tablespoons.

To make the meatloaf, beat the eggs in a large bowl and add the onion. Add the ground beef, oats, buttermilk, Worcestershire sauce, horseradish, salt, and pepper.

Mix together well (I just use my hands). Mix in the reserved 3 tablespoons of barbecue sauce.

Cut a large piece of heavy-duty aluminum foil (large enough to cover the inside of your slow cooker insert) and coat with cooking spray. Shape the meatloaf mixture into an oval and place it on top of the foil. Gently lift the foil and place it inside the slow cooker insert; open up the foil so the meatloaf is fully exposed. Cover the slow cooker and cook on low for 6 to 7 hours, until an instant-read thermometer inserted into the thickest part reads 160°F.

When the meatloaf is fully cooked, open the lid and generously brush on the barbecue sauce. Reserve any extra sauce for serving on the side. Cover and cook the meatloaf on low for another 30 minutes.

Lift the meatloaf from the pot, using the foil as handles, and let rest for at least 10 minutes. Cut into slices and serve with the extra barbecue sauce.

Pasta with West Virginia Three-Meat Gravy

This is an old family recipe from my Uncle DeMary's family in Fairmont, West Virginia. West Virginia is home to many Italian immigrants who crossed the pond to find work in the coal mines at the turn of the century. The descendents of these miners have kept their Italian heritage alive with dishes like pepperoni rolls, sausage and peppers, and, of course, Sunday pasta with gravy. This meaty, slow-cooked pasta sauce incorporates traditional Italian elements like home-made meatballs and Italian sausage, and there's also a subtle nod to our mountain roots with the addition of pan-fried cube steaks. Like any true all-day gravy, this recipe involves some extra prep (like making homemade meatballs and pan-frying the meats), but as you'll see, the end results are totally worth it and will certainly make *Nonna* proud.

Serves 10

MEATBALLS

¾ cup bread crumbs torn from a loaf of fresh bread, or ¼ cup fine dried bread crumbs

1½ pounds lean ground beef

3 tablespoons grated Parmesan cheese

2 tablespoons minced onion

2 cloves garlic, minced

2 eggs

1½ teaspoons dried parsley

½ teaspoon dried basil

½ teaspoon dried oregano

¼ teaspoon salt

¼ teaspoon black pepper

1½ teaspoons extra virgin olive oil

In a large bowl, mix the bread crumbs, ground beef, Parmesan cheese, onion, garlic, eggs, parsley, basil, oregano, salt, and pepper together with your hands and shape into balls about 2 inches in diameter.

Spray the slow cooker with cooking spray or coat the inside with olive oil.

Heat a large sauté pan over medium-high heat on the stovetop and add the olive oil. Add the meatballs and brown well on all sides, about 5 to 7 minutes. (To avoid overcrowding the pan, you may have to do this in batches.) Transfer the browned meatballs to the slow cooker as you finish cooking them. Do not wash the sauté pan.

ingredients and method continued

THREE-MEAT GRAVY

¼ cup all-purpose flour
⅛ teaspoon salt
⅛ teaspoon black pepper
1 pound cube steaks, cut into quarters
1 pound mild Italian sausage links
1½ teaspoons extra virgin olive oil
1 onion, chopped (about 1¼ cups)
6 large cloves garlic, minced
½ cup dry red wine
1 (8-ounce) can tomato sauce
2 (35-ounce) cans crushed tomatoes
1 cup water
1 tablespoon dried parsley
1 tablespoon dried oregano
1 tablespoon dried basil
2 bay leaves
¼ teaspoon dried red pepper flakes
1 tablespoon tomato paste
Salt and black pepper

2 pounds spaghetti or pasta of
    your choice
Fresh basil, shredded for garnish
    (optional)
Parmesan cheese, for serving

Combine the flour, salt, and pepper in a shallow dish and mix. Lightly toss the cube steak pieces in the flour and then brown in the oil remaining in the sauté pan over medium-high heat until crispy, about 6 to 8 minutes. Add the cube steaks to the slow cooker. Next, brown the sausages in the sauté pan, adding more oil if necessary, about 5 to 7 minutes, and add those to the slow cooker.

Add another 1½ teaspoons olive oil to the pan. Add the onion and garlic to the pan and sauté until translucent, about 5 to 6 minutes. Deglaze the pan with red wine and cook for 1 minute, scraping up any bits off the bottom of the pan. Pour this mixture into the slow cooker.

Add the tomato sauce, crushed tomatoes, water, parsley, oregano, basil, bay leaves, and red pepper to the slow cooker. Stir in the tomato paste. Give the ingredients one more stir, then cover and cook on low for at least 8 hours and up to 10 hours. Once the sauce is done, season with salt and pepper and remove the bay leaves before serving.

Cook the pasta until al dente in a large pot of salted boiling water. Drain.

To serve, pile the cooked pasta on a platter. Spoon some of the meatballs, sausages, and cubed steak around the spaghetti and sprinkle with fresh basil. Pour the remaining sauce into a large serving bowl or gravy boat. Set out a bowl of grated Parmesan cheese. Let guests serve themselves.

TO DRINK *The West Virginia Hound*

Arguably, pairing white whiskey (aka moonshine) with an Italian pasta dish is about as far out as one can get, but we mountain folk like to argue that moonshine goes with everything! Mixologist David Ortiz created this white lightening–style cocktail incorporating white whiskey made in the hills of West Virginia, which is a potent (and legal) blend of 100-proof hooch that its creators at Smooth Ambler Spirits like to refer to as "sophisticated moonshine." *Serves 1*

2 fluid ounces Smooth Ambler Exceptional White Whiskey
    or similar white or aged whiskey
¾ fluid ounce simple syrup
2 cucumber slices, plus more for garnish
Small handful of fresh cilantro, plus more for garnish
Crushed ice

Combine all the ingredients in a glass and muddle well. Add the mixture to a shaker with ice. Shake vigorously. Double strain into a rocks glass filled with crushed ice. Garnish with a cilantro leaf and cucumber slice.

Note: Simple syrup is a (simple!) mixture of 1 part sugar and 1 part water. To make a batch, combine 1 cup sugar and 1 cup water in a saucepan and bring it to a boil. Reduce the heat to a simmer and stir until the sugar dissolves, then remove from the heat and cool to room temperature. Stored in a jar in the fridge, the simple syrup will keep for up to a month.

Pork Loin Roast

WITH ROSEMARY, BALSAMIC VINEGAR, AND VANILLA FIG JAM

Throughout much of the South, fig trees abound. Those of us lucky enough to have some wait anxiously until that magical summer month when our bounty finally appears. One year we had a bumper crop of ripe, purple turkey figs, and I couldn't resist making a fig jam accented with rosemary, vanilla, and balsamic vinegar. While this easy-to-make jam tastes great on a biscuit, its flavors are elevated when paired with a slow-cooked pork roast doused in a rustic onion sauce. This is a dish made for entertaining, and it's perfect for an al fresco, end-of-summer dinner party. Got leftovers? Why not make Cuban sandwiches: butter two slices of bread, add mustard, dill pickles, pork, sliced ham, and Swiss cheese, then grill the sandwich in a cast-iron skillet.

Serves 8

FIG JAM

10 to 12 fresh figs, stems removed and flesh chopped (about 2 cups chopped)

¼ cup granulated sugar

¼ cup honey

2 tablespoons balsamic vinegar

¼ teaspoon vanilla bean paste or extract

1 teaspoon minced fresh rosemary

Pinch of cayenne pepper

1 (3- to 4-pound) boneless pork loin roast

1 teaspoon minced garlic

½ teaspoon minced fresh rosemary

¼ teaspoon salt, plus more to taste

⅛ teaspoon black pepper, plus more to taste

1 large onion, sliced (about 2 cups)

1 teaspoon all-purpose flour mixed to a paste with 1 teaspoon softened unsalted butter (*beurre manié*)

Combine all of the ingredients for the fig jam in a saucepan. Bring to a boil and simmer, uncovered, for 15 minutes, or until thickened. Set aside.

Spray the inside of the slow cooker with cooking spray. Trim any excess fat and silver skin off the pork roast. Rub the outside of the pork loin with the garlic, rosemary, salt, and pepper.

Put the onions in the slow cooker and lay the pork, fat side up, on top. Smother the pork well with the fig jam. Cover and cook on low for 6 to 8 hours, basting every couple of hours, if possible, until the internal temperature of the meat reads 145°F. Transfer the pork to a cutting board and let rest.

Meanwhile, pour the leftover pork juices and onions into a saucepan and bring to a boil. Once it reaches a boil, continue to cook over medium heat, uncovered, for 10 minutes. During the last minute or so, whisk in the flour and butter paste. Cook the sauce until slightly thickened. Season to taste with salt and pepper.

Slice the pork and place on a serving platter. Spoon the sauce over the pork and serve any extra sauce on the side.

TO DRINK Since this pork is both savory and sweet, I recommend serving it with a slightly tannic, fruity red wine, such as a Meritage blend. Virginia's King Family Vineyards' 2010 Meritage would be an excellent choice.

SoCo Baked City Ham

While we Southerners love our country ham, lately I've become quite the fan of "city ham." Unlike country ham, which is salted and dry cured, city hams are wet cured in a brine of salt, sugar, and spices and then smoked. The result is a more delicately flavored ham that doesn't need to be soaked (unlike country ham) before eating. City hams are often sold in halves and can be found at most grocery stores. They are a cinch to prepare since they are already pre-cooked and seasoned. All you need to do is rub the ham with the seasonings of your choice or spoon a simple glaze over it before cooking, or, as with this recipe, do a little bit of both. Since city hams are still a bit salty, they taste best when balanced with a sweet marinade or sugary dry rub. For this recipe, I've riffed on a classic Southern cocktail combo: SoCo (Southern Comfort) and cola. Of course, you can leave out the booze and add an extra ¼ cup of cola, if you like. • Most hams come with some fat still on. While keeping the layers of fat intact is essential when you're smoking ham, when you leave it on in the slow cooker, too much fat ends up getting rendered into the pot. With this in mind, I recommend cutting any visible fat back to ¼-inch or so, and then scoring it for presentation. You'll need a 6-quart or larger slow cooker for this recipe due to the size of the ham. Or you can use a smaller ham in a 4- or 5-quart cooker.

Serves 8 to 10

1 (4- to 5-pound) bone-in smoked "city" ham half
¼ cup firmly packed brown sugar
1 teaspoon dry mustard powder
1 teaspoon onion powder
¼ teaspoon ground allspice
½ teaspoon black pepper
1 cup cola (not diet)
¼ cup Southern Comfort
1½ teaspoons cider vinegar
1 tablespoon spicy brown mustard
Pineapple slices, for topping
Whole cloves (optional)

Remove the ham from the fridge and let it come close to room temperature. Rinse and pat dry. Trim the excess fat and skin off the ham, leaving about ¼ inch. Score the outside of the ham in a diagonal fashion in two directions to make diamond shapes.

Spray the inside of the slow cooker with cooking spray.

In a small bowl, mix together the brown sugar, dry mustard, onion powder, allspice, and black pepper. Rub this all over the ham, especially on the top. Place the ham fat side up inside the slow cooker. In the same bowl, whisk together the cola, Southern Comfort, cider vinegar, and brown mustard. Pour this over and around the ham. Be careful not to wash all the dry rub off the top of the ham since the crust is the best part. Skewer the pineapple slices to the top with cloves or toothpicks.

Cover and cook on low for at least 7 hours and up to 9 hours, basting the ham periodically with the sauce, until an internal temperature of the ham reads 140°F. Let the ham rest for at least 20 minutes before slicing and serving.

TO DRINK *Classic SoCo and Cola*

Southern Comfort originated in New Orleans in the late 1800s and is a unique blend of fruit, spices, and whiskey. It's great when mixed with other fruit juices and excellent with cola over ice. Vanilla-flavored cola or cherry cola is also delicious. *Serves 1*

Ice, preferably crushed
2 fluid ounces Southern Comfort
Cola (not diet)
Slice of orange
2 maraschino cherries, skewered on a toothpick

Fill a rocks glass with ice and pour in the Southern Comfort. Top with cola and give it quick stir. Garnish with the slice of orange and the maraschino cherries.

Dr. Pepper Sorghum Roasted Ham

This semi-boneless smoked ham is bathed in a glaze made from sorghum syrup, spices, and Dr. Pepper and will be a surefire hit for your next Sunday supper. Semi-boneless hams have the shank bone removed to make them easier to carve. Serve this sweet, salty ham with scalloped potatoes, green beans (page 80), and hot rolls (page 126), and don't forget to save your ham bone for cooking greens or beans. • If you have leftovers, you can also make ham salad: Just combine the ham in a food processor with a minced shallot, some mayonnaise, honey mustard, sweet pickle relish, whipped cream cheese, minced parsley, walnut pieces, and a chopped hard-boiled egg. Season with black pepper and serve over mini dinner rolls—delicious! • One last note: Make sure you buy a ham that will fit into your slow cooker. Many grocery stores and butchers sell semi-boneless, smoked ham halves, which are fully cooked, but not salt cured. Look for hams that are sold in their "natural juices" versus ones that have had a large percentage of water added, which dilutes flavor and overall quality.

Serves 6 to 8

1 (4- to 5-pound) semi-boneless, smoked ham half or spiral sliced ham

¼ cup sorghum syrup, unsulfured light molasses, or honey

¼ cup plus 1 tablespoon firmly packed brown sugar

½ teaspoon black pepper

¼ teaspoon ground cinnamon

¼ teaspoon ground nutmeg

Pinch of cayenne pepper

1 tablespoon cider vinegar

2 cups Dr. Pepper (not diet)

If you're using a smoked ham, rinse it and pat it dry (spiral sliced ham can be used as is). Trim off excess fat, leaving about ½ inch. Score the outside of the ham in a diagonal fashion in two directions to make diamond shapes.

Spray the inside of the slow cooker with cooking spray.

In a small bowl, whisk together the sorghum, ¼ cup of the brown sugar, black pepper, cinnamon, nutmeg, cayenne, and cider vinegar. Brush this mixture all over the ham. Place the ham, scored side up, in the slow cooker. Pour the Dr. Pepper down the sides of the cooker and around the ham (try not to wash off the glaze). Finally, sprinkle the remaining 1 tablespoon of brown sugar over the top of the ham and rub it into the meat.

Cover and cook the ham on low for at least 6 hours and up to 8 hours, basting with the cooking liquid occasionally (a turkey baster works well for this), until an instant-read thermometer reads 140°F. Be careful not to overcook the ham, or it will dry out.

Transfer the ham to a large serving platter. Carve and serve.

There is a doctor in the house, and his name is Craig Mrusek, a booze columnist and bartender (aka Dr. Bamboo). Craig was named one of "The 25 Most Influential Online Cocktail Pioneers" in the book *Vintage Spirits & Forgotten Cocktails*. He was kind enough to create this whimsical cocktail recipe, which incorporates bourbon mixed with a homemade Dr. Pepper syrup and fresh muddled thyme. Serve this soda pop–style cocktail on the rocks with an orange peel slice. *Serves 1*

1 tablespoon Dr. Pepper syrup (see below)
2 to 3 sprigs fresh thyme
2 fluid ounces bourbon, preferably a robust-tasting brand,
   such as Bulleit or Buffalo Trace
Ice cubes
Orange peel, for garnish

To make the Dr. Pepper syrup, pour 3 cups Dr. Pepper into a small saucepan and simmer over medium low heat, stirring frequently, until it reduces and thickens to a syrup-like consistency, about 30 minutes. You'll end up with approximately 5 to 6 fluid ounces of syrup. Store unused syrup in a glass container with a tight-fitting lid for up to a week.

In a cocktail shaker, muddle together 1 tablespoon of the Dr. Pepper syrup and thyme. Add the bourbon and ice and shake well. Strain into an ice-filled rocks glass and garnish with a thick strip of orange peel.

Graham Cracker–Stuffed Ham Steaks

One of my prized possessions is my grandmother's collection of community cookbooks, which is where I found the inspiration for this recipe. The original recipe was for a ham loaf—meatloaf made with ground ham instead of beef. It incorporated graham cracker crumbs as a binder instead of plain, old bread crumbs. I just had to give it a try, so borrowing on the same idea, I created this recipe for ham steaks stuffed with a sweet and savory graham cracker stuffing. The combination of salty pan-fried ham with brown sugar, crushed graham crackers, and molasses is definitely one that will keep the kids happy. Serve with green beans (page 80) and creamed new potatoes (page 81).

Serves 4 to 6

1 large onion, sliced

2 tablespoons pineapple juice, reserved from a can of pineapple rings

2 (8-ounce) center-cut ham steaks, about 1 pound each, trimmed of excess fat

1 teaspoon vegetable oil

1 cup fresh bread crumbs

1 cup graham cracker crumbs

¼ cup chopped walnuts

1½ teaspoons light molasses

1 egg, beaten

1½ teaspoons brown sugar

¼ teaspoon ground cinnamon

⅛ teaspoon cloves

Pinch of black pepper

2 tablespoons milk

½ teaspoon cider vinegar

Sliced pineapple rings

1 tablespoon unsalted butter, cut into small pieces

Line the slow cooker with heavy-duty aluminum foil all the way up the sides of the insert and cut to fit. Spray the foil generously with cooking spray. Put the sliced onions in the slow cooker and pour in the pineapple juice.

Pat dry and score the outside fat layer of the ham steaks. Add vegetable oil to a large cast-iron pan and heat to medium-high. Add the steaks, in batches if necessary, and pan-fry on both sides until browned, about 3 to 4 minutes per side.

While the ham steaks are browning, mix together bread crumbs, graham cracker crumbs, walnuts, molasses, egg, brown sugar, cinnamon, cloves, black pepper, milk, and cider vinegar.

Lay one ham steak on top of the onions. Then spoon the graham cracker filling on top of the ham steak and press it into the meat. Top with the other ham steak. Top with 3 or 4 pineapple rings, for garnish, and then dot with butter.

Cover and cook on low for at least 5 hours and up to 6½ hours. Remove the ham steaks and stuffing by lifting them out by the foil handles. Let rest for 6 to 8 minutes. Cut into serving pieces and drizzle with the remaining juices from the pot.

TO DRINK A slightly sweet and spicy Gewürztraminer, such as the one from White Hall Vineyards of Virginia

Pork Ribs

WITH RASPBERRY SORGHUM BBQ SAUCE

These ribs incorporate two distinct cooking methods. First, the ribs are rubbed in a dry spice mixture, then cooked all day until tender. Next, they're slathered in a sweet and savory barbecue sauce made from fresh raspberries and sorghum syrup before they finally meet a hot grill. However, no worries if you're not able to get your grill going. An equally tasty alternative is to brush the ribs with the barbecue sauce right in the slow cooker, then cover, crank the heat up to high and continue cooking for another 30 minutes. Either way, at the end of the day, you'll have a delicious, sticky, messy, lick-your-fingers-clean rack of ribs that will be a sure-fire hit. • I recommend using a 5- or 6-quart slow cooker for this recipe so you can comfortably fit all the ribs. If you can't find sorghum, substitute light molasses. This sauce is also excellent with grilled chicken, pork chops, or grilled pork loin.

Serves 4 to 6

DRY RUB
1½ tablespoons onion powder
1½ tablespoons brown sugar
1 tablespoon chili powder
1 tablespoon salt
1½ teaspoons black pepper
1 teaspoon dry mustard powder
¼ teaspoon cayenne pepper

2 racks of pork spareribs or one large
   rack (about 4 pounds), trimmed

SAUCE
1½ cups fresh raspberries
   (blackberries may be substituted)
2 small cloves garlic, chopped
½ cup chopped onion
½ cup firmly packed brown sugar
½ cup sorghum syrup, unsulfured
   light molasses, or honey
½ cup ketchup
1 tablespoon cider vinegar
1 teaspoon powdered ginger
¼ teaspoon dried red pepper flakes
Salt and black pepper

Spray the inside of the slow cooker with cooking spray.

Mix all your dry rub ingredients together in a small bowl. Cut the ribs into 2- to 3-rib portions to fit inside the slow cooker. Generously rub the ribs with the spice mixture and stand them up against the walls of the slower cooker, thicker ends down. Cover and cook on low for at least 5 hours and up to 7 hours, until the ribs are tender but still firm enough to hold up on the grill without falling apart; be careful not to overcook them.

Meanwhile, make the sauce. Combine in a blender the raspberries, garlic, onion, brown sugar, sorghum syrup, ketchup, cider vinegar, ginger, and red pepper flakes. Purée well. Strain the sauce through a sieve (pressing it out well) into a saucepan and cook, uncovered, over low heat for 30 minutes, or until thickened. Season to taste with salt and pepper and set aside to cool. (Note: You can skip straining the sauce through a sieve if you don't mind the seeds.)

Once the ribs have finished cooking, preheat a grill to medium-high.

continued

Pork Ribs with Raspberry Sorghum BBQ Sauce, continued

Baste the ribs generously with the sauce and grill them until nice and crispy and caramelized, 3 to 4 minutes per side; be careful not to let them burn. Alternatively, sauce the ribs inside the slow cooker and continue cooking on high, as mentioned in the headnote. Serve the ribs with any extra sauce on the side and lots of napkins.

TO DRINK   A fruity beer, such as a Lambic; or Hardywood Park Craft Brewery's Virginia Blackberry from Richmond, Virginia

Trimming Ribs An easy way to remove the tough membrane from a rack of spareribs is to gently slide a butter knife underneath the membrane to release it. Then, grab the membrane with a paper towel and start pulling it back, working it away from the bone.

Country-Style Pork Ribs
WITH BOURBON AND COKE BBQ SAUCE

Country-style ribs are not actually ribs. This cut of meat comes from the shoulder of the pig, where it is sliced in half under the blade bone and then cut into long strips to resemble ribs. As a result, much like other tough cuts of meat, country-style ribs benefit from any type of low and slow cooking. Tender, tangy, and accented with just a hint of bourbon, these ribs are a messy, saucy affair. Bone-in country-style ribs are recommended for this recipe since it's the bones that are packed with the most flavor (you can use boneless ribs, but they may require less cooking time).

Serves 6 to 8

4 to 5 pounds bone-in pork country-style ribs

Salt and black pepper

1 tablespoon vegetable oil

1½ cups ketchup

½ cup cola (not diet)

3 tablespoons tomato paste

2 cloves garlic, minced

2 tablespoons brown sugar

2 tablespoons American spicy ketchup-based sauce (such as Heinz brand chili sauce) or homemade chili sauce (page 61)

2 tablespoons good-quality bourbon

2 tablespoons cider vinegar

1 tablespoon sorghum syrup or light molasses

1 teaspoon Worcestershire sauce

1 teaspoon chili powder

¼ teaspoon cayenne pepper

Trim any excess fat from the ribs and cut into approximately 5-inch-long pieces. Lightly season the ribs with salt and pepper.

Heat a large sauté pan on the stovetop over medium-high heat. Add the oil, then the ribs, and brown well on all sides. (To avoid overcrowding the pan, you may have to do this in batches.)

While the ribs are searing, spray the inside of the slow cooker with cooking spray. Add the ketchup, cola, tomato paste, garlic, brown sugar, chili sauce, bourbon, cider vinegar, sorghum syrup, Worcestershire sauce, chili powder, and cayenne. Stir well. Add the ribs to the slow cooker, layering the larger fattier ribs on the bottom. Make sure all the ribs are covered in sauce. Cover and cook on low for at least 8 hours and up to 9 hours, until the meat is fall-off-the-bone tender.

Transfer the ribs to a platter and keep warm. Pour the leftover sauce into a small saucepan and cook over medium heat for 10 to 15 minutes, until it is reduced and slightly thickened. Skim off any visible fat, season with salt and pepper, and serve the sauce over the ribs.

Cocktail Wienies with Grape Jelly–Chili Sauce

The wild and wonderful combination of grape jelly, homemade chili sauce, and mini smoky cocktail links is no stranger to the Southern kitchen. At any given potluck, it's not uncommon to see several slow cookers simmering with some version of this recipe. While a mixture of sausage links and grape jelly might sound strange at first, trust me, this dish is a hit, and this recipe goes beyond any of the usual hot nibbles by incorporating homemade chili sauce versus using the jarred stuff. What results is a unique blend of sweet, spicy, and piquant, simply made for cocktail-party fare. Serve your wienies straight from the slow cooker (set on warm) with toothpicks. • It's worth noting that the chili sauce on its own is a great addition to ground beef when making sloppy joe's and is an excellent base for beef or bean chili.

Serves 12 to 15 as an appetizer

CHILI SAUCE
¼ cup cider vinegar
¼ cup firmly packed brown sugar
¼ teaspoon salt, plus more to taste
1¾ cups pureed tomatoes or
  tomato sauce
2 tablespoons tomato paste
⅓ cup chopped onion
¼ cup chopped green bell pepper
½ small jalapeño, seeded and minced
½ cinnamon stick
½ teaspoon whole cloves
1 bay leaf
Salt and black pepper

2 cups grape jelly
2 (14-ounce) packages smoked mini
  cocktail links (such as Lit'l Smokies)

Spray a slow cooker with cooking spray.

To make the chili sauce, combine cider vinegar, brown sugar, salt, tomatoes, tomato paste, onion, green bell pepper, and jalapeño in the slow cooker and stir well. Cut a small piece of cheese cloth and make a sachet to hold the cinnamon stick, cloves, and bay leaf. Add the sachet with the spices to the slow cooker, cover, and cook on low for 6 hours, stirring every couple of hours, so the sides don't burn. Then turn down to warm for 1 more hour. Remove the spice sachet and season to taste with salt and pepper.

Add the grape jelly and sausage links to the slow cooker, and stir to cover them with the sauce. Cover the slow cooker and cook on low for an additional 1 to 2 hours or until the grape jelly has melted and the sausages are fully heated through. Set the slow cooker to warm until ready to serve. Serve the links straight from the pot with toothpicks.

TO DRINK   A brown ale, such as Alabama Back Forty Beer Company's Truck Stop Honey Brown Ale

Carolina-Style Pork BBQ Sandwiches

Arguably, some of the best 'cue in the country can be found in North Carolina, where two distinct types of slow-cooked pig prevail. The first is Eastern barbecue, which is distinguished by slow-cooking a whole hog and including both the white and dark meat in chopped sandwiches and platters. Eastern 'cue boasts just a hint of vinegar and red pepper, which is added to the meat mix rather than used as a sauce. Western North Carolina 'cue (aka Lexington-style) is made from pork shoulder only. In addition to incorporating plenty of vinegar, sugar, and spices, it also mixes in a good amount of ketchup to create an actual sauce for the pork. This slow-cooker recipe falls somewhere in between. If you like, you can skip the sauce altogether and enjoy a basic roasted pork, which is not only fantastic on a bun with slaw (see recipe page 64) and hot sauce, but is great for making burritos, barbecue pizza, or nachos. I recommend using a 5- to 6-quart slow cooker for this recipe in order to comfortably fit the pork shoulder. You can also cut this recipe in half and use a smaller slow cooker.

Serves 10 to 12 (about 8 cups of meat)

2 large onions, sliced

5-pound boneless pork shoulder roast

6 cloves garlic, smashed

1 teaspoon salt

½ teaspoon black pepper

2 tablespoons brown sugar

1½ teaspoons dried red pepper flakes

1 cup cider vinegar

1 cup apple cider or apple juice

SAUCE

2 cups cooking liquid (reserved from the slow-cooked pork)

½ cup water

¼ cup ketchup

¼ cup cider vinegar

2 teaspoons brown sugar

1½ teaspoons Worcestershire sauce

1½ teaspoons chili powder

1 teaspoon paprika

1 teaspoon dry mustard powder

¼ teaspoon red pepper flakes

Salt and black pepper

Buns, slaw (page 64), and hot sauce, for serving

Spray the inside of a slow cooker with cooking spray.

Put the onions in the slow cooker. Make slits in the pork roast and insert the garlic cloves. Rub salt, pepper, brown sugar, and red pepper flakes into the meat. Place the pork in the slow cooker fat side up and pour in the vinegar and apple cider. Cover and cook on low for at least 10 hours and up to 12 hours, until the meat is falling-apart tender.

Transfer the meat to a large bowl and shred it with two forks. Set aside.

Pour 2 cups of the pan juices into a measuring cup; discard any leftover juices still in the pot. Let cool and skim off any visible fat. Pour this liquid into a saucepan. Add the water, ketchup, cider vinegar, brown sugar, Worcestershire sauce, chili powder, paprika, dry mustard, and red pepper flakes. Bring to a boil and simmer, uncovered, for 10 minutes. Season with salt and pepper. Return the shredded pork to the slow cooker and add 1 cup of the sauce mixture (more if you like it wet). Give it a stir and set the slow cooker to warm until ready to serve.

Serve the pork straight from the slow cooker with a slotted spoon, along with buns, slaw, and hot sauce. Serve the additional sauce on the side.

TO DRINK A tall glass of Southern-style iced sweet tea (heavy on the sugar)

West Virginia Slaw Dogs

My family back in West Virginia takes hotdogs very seriously. For starters, the chili that tops our dogs is known as "sauce," and it must contain at least a pinch of cinnamon and nary a bean in order to be the real deal. Unlike many traditional hot dog chili sauces, this one is made without any tomato sauce, tomato paste, or ketchup. As a result, this chili sauce is more of a piquant ground beef topping (rather than a thickened, stew-like chili). While it's fantastic spooned on a hotdog, it's also great for tacos and nachos, *and* you can use it as a base for making a more traditional chili (just add beans and tomato sauce). To make a real-deal West Virginia-style hotdog, top your chili dog with creamy slaw, onions, and a smear of yellow mustard.

Makes 3 cups chili sauce, enough for 12 hotdogs

CHILI SAUCE
1 tablespoon vegetable shortening
2 tablespoons diced onion
2 small cloves garlic, minced
1½ pounds extra-lean ground beef
1 tablespoon chili powder
1 tablespoon paprika
1½ teaspoons ground cumin
1½ teaspoons black pepper
1½ teaspoons salt
¼ teaspoon cayenne pepper
⅛ teaspoon ground cinnamon
2½ cups hot water

SLAW
¼ cup sugar, or to taste
3 tablespoons cider vinegar, or to taste
2 to 4 tablespoons mayonnaise
½ head cabbage, finely grated
Salt and black pepper
Pinch of celery seeds (optional)

12 all-beef hotdogs
12 hotdog buns
Yellow mustard, for serving
Diced onions, for serving

Spray the inside of the slow cooker with cooking spray.

Melt the shortening in a large sauté pan on the stovetop over medium-high heat. Add the onion and garlic and sauté until soft, about 5 minutes. Add the beef, breaking it up into little pieces, and brown well, about 7 to 8 minutes. Add the chili powder, paprika, cumin, black pepper, salt, cayenne, cinnamon, and ½ cup of the water and cook for 10 minutes. Transfer the mixture to the slow cooker, add the remaining 2 cups water, and stir. Cover and cook on low for at least 7 hours and up to 9 hours.

Meanwhile, make the slaw. In a large bowl, whisk together the sugar and vinegar until the sugar is completely dissolved. Add the mayo and mix the dressing until it is smooth and creamy. Add the cabbage, salt, pepper, and celery seeds and mix. Cover and chill for at least 45 minutes.

When the chili sauce is ready, steam or grill the hotdogs, then steam or grill the buns. Slather a bit of yellow mustard on the inside of each bun. Then (in order) add the hotdog, spoon on the hotdog sauce with a slotted spoon (so you don't soak your bun with too much liquid), sprinkle with onion, and finally top with a good spread of creamy slaw.

TO DRINK An American blonde-style ale, such as Mountain State Brewing Company's Cold Trail Ale, made in West Virginia

Red Beans and Rice with Smoked Sausage

Red beans and rice is a popular Creole dish, with culinary roots that traveled along the slave trade routes into Louisiana. Soul satisfying and heavily spiced (with hot peppers or hot sauce, traditionally added after cooking), slow-cooked red beans were often flavored with a ham bone leftover from Sunday supper and cooked on Mondays for a "wash day" or laundry day meal that required minimal attention while it simmered on the stove. Louisiana red beans are basically the same as kidney beans except they're smaller and rounder. For this recipe, I've replaced the ham bone with smoky sausage (or you can use andouille) and added plenty of Creole-style seasonings. Serve this dish over hot cooked rice with green onions and plenty of hot sauce for shaking.

Serves 6

2 cups dried red beans or kidney beans

½ teaspoon vegetable oil

1 pound smoked sausage or andouille sausage, if you like things spicy, sliced

4 cups chicken broth, low sodium or homemade (page 122), plus more if needed

1 small onion, chopped

½ cup chopped celery

3 cloves garlic, minced

1 teaspoon Worcestershire sauce

1 teaspoon Creole seasoning, such as Tony Chatchere's, or Cajun seasoning

1 teaspoon bacon grease (optional)

2 bay leaves

¼ teaspoon smoked paprika

¼ teaspoon dried thyme

Pinch of cayenne pepper (optional)

Water (as needed)

Salt and black pepper

Cooked rice, for serving

Minced green onions (white and green parts), for garnish

Hot sauce, for serving

Rinse and pick through the beans, discarding any debris. Put the beans in a large bowl, cover them with water by at least 2 inches, and soak overnight. Rinse and drain.

Spray the inside of the slow cooker with cooking spray.

Heat a large skillet on the stovetop over medium-high heat. Add the oil and sausage and cook the sausage until browned, 4 to 5 minutes. Pour the sausage and any renderings into the slow cooker. Add broth, onion, celery, garlic, Worcestershire sauce, Creole seasoning, bacon grease, bay leaves, smoked paprika, thyme, and cayenne. Add the beans and stir well. Cover and cook on low for at least 8 hours and up to 10 hours, adding more broth or water if necessary to keep the beans covered, until the beans are tender.

Turn the slow cooker to high, uncover the pot, and remove 1 to 2 cups of the beans (depending on how thick you want your stew) and mash them well with a fork or a potato masher. Return the mashed beans to the slow cooker. Continue cooking the beans, uncovered, on high for 1 hour, until the sauce has reduced and thickened.

Season with salt and pepper and remove the bay leaves. Serve the beans over hot cooked rice and sprinkle with green onions. Pass the hot sauce at the table.

TO DRINK   An icy cold mug of NOLA Brewing's 7th Street Wheat Beer from Louisiana, or a similar wheat brew

Cabbage with Smoked Sausage and Apples

This is my Southern slow-cooker answer to a French *choucroute garnie*, an Alsatian dish made with sauerkraut and various sausages, bacon, or pork belly cooked with white wine, juniper berries, Dijon mustard, potatoes, and perhaps a smidgen of duck fat. It's a stick-to-your-ribs kind of meal meant to be savored in front of a roaring fire with a glass of Riesling. I've given this version just a hint of Southern flavor with the addition of bacon fat, cider vinegar, and brown sugar. You can even toss in some peeled, cubed potatoes if you like. Serve this dish with an array of mustards and slices of dark rye bread for a complete meal. If you want a particularly meaty meal, increase the sausage to 2 pounds. • Juniper berries, which come from evergreen shrubs, can be found at spice shops, many organic groceries, kitchen stores, or can be purchased online at sites such as myspicesage.com.

Serves 4 to 6

1 head green cabbage, thinly sliced
1 onion, chopped
2 small (or one large) Granny Smith apples, cored and chopped
1 teaspoon bacon grease (optional)
1 clove garlic, minced
1 bay leaf
4 juniper berries, lightly crushed
3 tablespoons cider vinegar
1 tablespoon brown sugar
1 tablespoon whole-grain mustard
Generous pinch of caraway seeds
1 pound smoked sausage links, halved
Salt and black pepper

Spray the inside of the slow cooker with cooking spray.

Add the cabbage, onion, apples, bacon grease, garlic, bay leaf, juniper berries, cider vinegar, brown sugar, mustard, and caraway to the slow cooker. Stir well. Nestle the sausage pieces in the cabbage mixture, so they don't dry out. Cover and cook on low, stirring the cabbage mixture every now and then, for at least 6 hours and up to 8 hours. Season with salt and pepper and serve.

TO DRINK *The Man Named Curtis Sloe*

Richmond, Virginia, mixologist Mattias Hagglund created this playful, potent cocktail incorporating sloe gin (a ruby colored liqueur made from blackthorn berries) with lemon juice, a little sugar, bitters, and a dash of sparkling seltzer. It is as lovely to look at as it is to sip. *Serves 1*

1 fluid ounce Wild Turkey rye or other rye whiskey
1 fluid ounce Plymouth sloe gin or other sloe gin
1½ tablespoons fresh lemon juice
1½ tablespoons simple syrup (see note on page 49)
3 dashes of Angostura bitters
Ice
1 fluid ounce seltzer
Twist of orange, for garnish

Fill a cocktail shaker with ice and add the rye, sloe gin, lemon juice, simple syrup, and bitters. Shake well and strain into a rocks glass filled with ice. Top with the seltzer. Garnish with a twist of orange.

Chicken with Maple Cider White BBQ Sauce

Dry-rubbed, tender cooked chicken thighs meet a creamy Alabama-inspired barbecue white sauce made from mayonnaise, cider vinegar, and just a smidgin of maple syrup for sweetness. Originally created in 1925 by "Big Bob" Gibson of Big Bob Gibson's Bar B-Q in Decatur, Alabama, this highly versatile sauce is almost as much of a condiment as it is a sauce for pork and chicken. Try brushing it on a piece of grilled fish, adding It to a homemade potato salad, or serving it as a dip for fresh vegetables.

Serves 4 to 6

DRY RUB

1 tablespoon chili powder
1 tablespoon onion powder
1 teaspoon garlic powder
½ teaspoon cayenne pepper
1 teaspoon dry mustard powder
1 tablespoon sweet paprika
½ teaspoon ground allspice
¼ teaspoon salt
¾ teaspoon black pepper

1 large onion, sliced
8 bone-in, skinless chicken thighs
½ cup chicken broth, low sodium or
    unsalted homemade (page 122)

SAUCE

1¼ cups mayonnaise
2 tablespoons cider vinegar
¼ cup pure maple syrup
¼ teaspoon prepared horseradish
⅛ teaspoon salt
½ teaspoon black pepper
Couple of dashes of hot sauce,
    such as Crystal

In a small bowl, mix together the dry rub ingredients.

Spray the inside of the slow cooker with cooking spray. Add the sliced onions.

Generously rub the mixture into the chicken and place the chicken in the slow cooker. Pour in the chicken broth. Cover and cook on low for at least 5 hours and up to 6 hours, until tender.

Meanwhile, whisk together the BBQ sauce ingredients in a bowl. Cover and chill until ready to use.

Transfer the chicken to a platter and serve with the white sauce for dipping.

TO DRINK *Maple Mint Julep*

Cocktail expert and poet, Autumn Giles, who blogs at "Autumn Makes and Does" has kindly shared her recipe for a mint julep. She adds a slight twist to this classic with the addition of pure maple syrup, which I find to be an excellent pairing with this chicken dish. *Serves 1*

10 fresh mint leaves, plus a sprig for garnish
1 tablespoon maple syrup
2 fluid ounces good-quality bourbon
Crushed ice

Muddle the mint leaves and maple syrup in the bottom of an old-fashioned glass. Fill the glass ¾ full with crushed ice. Pour the bourbon over the ice and stir to combine. Top with additional ice, if desired, and stir. Serve garnished with a sprig of fresh mint.

Dry Mustard–Rubbed Shredded Chicken

After making this recipe, you just might forgo buying store-bought rotisserie chickens. Not only is this slow-cooker chicken super easy, but it makes plenty of shredded meat that's perfect for making homemade chicken salad, filling burritos, stuffing pot pies, or making off-the-cuff barbecue sandwiches (just mix with your favorite barbecue sauce). Leftover shredded chicken can also be frozen. Just pack in individual freezer bags and cover with chicken broth to prevent freezer burn. Thaw the meat in the fridge and then strain off the broth before using.

Serves 8

1 (4- to 5-pound) whole chicken

DRY RUB
¼ cup dry mustard powder
1½ tablespoons chili powder
1 tablespoon garlic powder
1 tablespoon onion powder
1 tablespoon brown sugar
2 teaspoons dried thyme
2 teaspoons salt
1 teaspoon white pepper
¼ teaspoon cayenne pepper

1 large sweet onion, sliced
3 large carrots, cut into pieces
4 celery stalks, cut into pieces
1 bay leaf

Rinse the chicken inside and out. Pat dry. Mix all of the dry rub ingredients in a small bowl and rub the chicken inside and out with the mixture. Be sure to push some of the dry rub up under the skin.

Spray the inside of the slow cooker with cooking spray. Layer the onion, carrots, celery, and bay leaf in the slow cooker. Place the chicken, breast-side up, on top of the vegetables. Cover and cook on low for 8 hours, basting it occasionally with any pan juices, until the chicken is falling-off-the-bone tender.

Transfer the chicken to a large bowl. Let cool and remove the meat. Save the leftover bones, carcass, and skin and any leftover vegetables for making chicken stock (see page 122) or discard. Use the meat immediately in your favorite recipe or store in the freezer.

TO DRINK Semi-oaked Chardonnay such as Veritas Winery's Harlequin Reserve Chardonnay from Virginia

Cornish Game Hens
WITH APPLE BUTTER BBQ SAUCE

Cornish game hens, also known as Rock Cornish hens, are actually domesticated chickens (*not* actual game meat). They are much smaller than standard chickens, ranging in size from 1½ to 2 pounds each. Because of their smaller size, Cornish hens make for a lovely presentation and can either be served whole (smaller hens) or sliced in half. When it comes to cooking Cornish hens in the slow cooker, I recommend using a 6-quart, which can fit two or more hens, depending on their size. This recipe incorporates a homemade barbecue sauce made from apple butter, which is an excellent way to use up any leftover slow-cooker apple butter (page 118). Serve the hens with new potatoes (page 81) and potato rolls (page 126).

Serves 2 to 4

1 tablespoon canola or vegetable oil
2 pounds Rock Cornish game hens
    (about 2 hens, depending on size)
    thawed, rinsed, and patted dry
    inside and out
1 cup chopped onion
1 cup peeled and chopped apples
1 tablespoon chopped fresh sage
    leaves

DRY RUB
¼ teaspoon salt
½ teaspoon black pepper
Pinch of cayenne pepper
¼ teaspoon dried thyme
¼ teaspoon garlic powder
½ teaspoon chili powder
¼ teaspoon paprika
1 teaspoon minced fresh sage leaves,
    or ¼ teaspoon dried

½ cup apple cider

Spray the inside of the slow cooker with cooking spray.

Heat a large sauté pan on the stovetop over medium-high heat and add the oil. When the oil begins to shimmer, place the game hens, breast-sides down, in the pan. Brown the hens well on all sides, about 4 minutes per side, and then transfer them to a platter or cutting board. Fill the cavity of each hen with the onion, apples, and sage.

In a small bowl, mix together the dry rub ingredients. Rub the dry rub into and up under the skin of the game hens and the place them in the slow cooker, breast-side up. Pour the apple cider around the hens. Cover the slow cooker and cook on low for at least 4 hours and up to 5 hours, until the interior of the meat registers 180°F on an instant-read thermometer.

SAUCE

¾ cup apple butter
½ cup ketchup
½ teaspoon minced garlic
1 tablespoon light molasses
2 teaspoons brown sugar
1 teaspoon cider vinegar
½ teaspoon Worcestershire sauce
Salt and black pepper

Meanwhile, in a saucepan, mix together all of the BBQ sauce ingredients. Bring to a simmer, reduce the heat to medium-low, and continue to cook for 10 minutes. Set aside.

When your game hens are fully cooked, brush them generously with the BBQ sauce, reserving any extra sauce for serving on the side. Cover and crank the slow cooker up to high and continue cooking the hens for 20 more minutes. Serve the hens with the extra BBQ sauce on the side.

TO DRINK *The Screen Porch*

Southerners love their Cheerwine soda, an addictive, bubbly, cherry-infused beverage made in Salisbury, North Carolina. Award-winning mixologist Thomas T. Leggett of The Roosevelt restaurant in Richmond, Virginia pays homage to this delightful drink (also known as "the Nectar of North Carolina") by mixing it with gin, St. Germain (an elderflower liqueur), and a splash of fresh lemon juice. *Serves 1*

1½ ounces gin
½ ounce St. Germain
½ ounce fresh lemon juice
Cheerwine soda (or cherry-flavored Dr. Pepper)
Slice of fresh lime, for garnish

Combine the gin, St. Germain, and lemon juice in a shaker with ice. Shake well, then strain into Collins glass filled with ice. Top with the Cheerwine and garnish with a slice of lime.

Herbed Turkey with Cornbread Dressing

This almost-all-in-one slow-cooker turkey dinner is Thanksgiving in a pot. All you need to finish it off is some cranberry sauce and gravy. Instead of stuffing the dressing into the bird, spread a buttery cornbread mixture on the bottom of the slow cooker where it collects all of those precious turkey drippings as it cooks. (Since it's technically not going *into* the bird, I'm calling this a dressing, not stuffing). This recipe also involves making a simple compound herb butter that is massaged into the turkey breast for added flavor and moisture. Be sure to watch the salt with this one because many grocery store turkey breasts already contain a good amount of sodium. And be sure to make turkey sandwiches with the leftovers!

Serves 4 to 6

1 (8-ounce) package cubed cornbread stuffing mix

½ cup diced celery

½ cup diced onion

2 tablespoons unsalted butter, melted

1 teaspoon dried poultry seasoning

1 cup chicken broth, low sodium or homemade (page 122)

1 tablespoon unsalted butter, softened

½ teaspoon dried sage, or 1 tablespoon fresh minced sage

½ teaspoon dried thyme

¼ teaspoon black pepper

1 (3- to 4-pound) boneless turkey breast, thawed

In a large bowl, mix together the cornbread stuffing mix, celery, onion, melted butter, poultry seasoning, and chicken broth.

Spray the inside of the slow cooker with cooking spray and spread the dressing mixture along the bottom.

In a small bowl, mix together 1 tablespoon softened butter, sage, thyme, and black pepper. Set aside.

Remove the turkey breast from its packaging. Remove the gravy packet, if there is one. Rinse the turkey and pat dry. Carefully cut away the netting that surrounds the breast. (This may cause the turkey to split apart; just press it back together.) With a sharp knife or kitchen shears, cut away the larger pieces of visible fat from the turkey breast, leaving a thin layer on top of the breast. Place the turkey skin side up in the slow cooker on top of the dressing mix.

Rub the herb butter mixture all over the turkey, pushing it up under the skin and coating it well. Press any loose pieces or turkey back together to form an oval shape.

Cover and cook on low for at least 4½ hours and up to 5 hours, until an instant-read thermometer inserted into the thickest part of the turkey reads 165°F. About halfway through cooking, give the dressing a stir or two for more even cooking.

Transfer the turkey to a cutting board and let rest for 10 minutes. Stir the dressing gently and cook on high for another 10 to 12 minute for a drier, fluffier dressing. (Note: you can skip this step if you like a moist dressing.)

Cut the turkey into slices and serve over the dressing.

TO DRINK *The Danville Rattlesnake*

Danville, Virginia–raised mixologist Thomas T. Leggett knows his stuff when it comes to bourbon-based cocktails. The Danville Rattlesnake, which gets its punch from the addition of mezcal (a Mexican spirit distilled from agave) is classic Southern, with just the right amount of South-of-the-Border flair. This one will sneak up and bite you if you're not careful! *Serves 1*

1½ ounces bourbon (such as Old Grand-Dad brand)
½ ounce mezcal (such as Del Maguey Vida brand)
¾ ounce fresh lemon juice
¾ ounce simple syrup (see Note on page 49)
2 dashes peach or Angostura bitters
Orange peel, to garnish

Combine the bourbon, mezcal, lemon juice, simple syrup, and bitters in a shaker filled with ice. Shake well, then strain into an ice-filled rocks glass and garnish with the orange peel.

Shrimp Creole

Louisiana Creole cooking has a diverse array of influences, which includes the influence of European settlers who came to New Orleans, specifically those from Spain, France, and Germany. Today, Creole cooking is an amalgamation of various cultures and culinary stylings, from French-style bouillabaisse and German-style cured meats to West Indian slow-cooked gumbos and Spanish-style spiced rice and meat dishes. Jambalaya, which is similar to paella, as well as this recipe for shrimp cooked with tomatoes, green pepper, and spices exemplifies the Spanish influence. This particular slow-cooker version of shrimp Creole involves simmering the sauce for up to 8 hours and adding the shrimp at the very end, so they don't overcook. Serve this spicy Creole dish over steamed rice garnished with green onions.

Serves 6

1 tablespoon unsalted butter
1 tablespoon extra virgin olive oil
1 cup chopped onion
½ cup chopped celery
4 small cloves garlic, minced
1 (16-ounce) can diced tomatoes
    with its juice
1 (8-ounce) can tomato sauce
¼ teaspoon dried thyme
1 teaspoon sugar
1 teaspoon Worcestershire sauce
1 teaspoon chili powder
¼ teaspoon salt, plus more to taste
¼ teaspoon cayenne pepper,
    or more to taste
2 bay leaves
½ cup diced green bell pepper
1 pound medium-size shrimp, peeled
    and deveined
Salt and black pepper
Steamed long-grain rice, for serving
Minced chives or green onions,
    for garnish
Hot sauce, for serving

Spray the inside of the slow cooker with cooking spray.

Heat the butter and olive oil in a cast-iron pan over medium-high heat. Add the onion and celery and sauté for 3 to 4 minutes, or until translucent. Add the garlic and sauté for another minute. Transfer the onion, celery, and garlic to the slow cooker and add the tomatoes, tomato sauce, thyme, sugar, Worcestershire sauce, chili powder, salt, cayenne, and bay leaves. Cover and cook on low for at least 6 hours and up to 8 hours.

One hour before serving, add the bell pepper and continue to cook on low. Finally, during the last 10 minutes, add the shrimp and cook until they are pink and slightly curled (be careful not to overcook). Season with salt and pepper. Remove the bay leaf and spoon over rice. Garnish with a sprinkling of fresh chives. Serve with hot sauce on the side.

TO DRINK A dry, fruity rosé, such as Pontchartrain Vineyards Zydeco Rosato from Louisiana

CHAPTER THREE

Vegetables and Sides

In Praise of the Vegetable Plate

Vegetables of all sorts are a staple on any down-home Southern table, and country folk are more than happy to make a meal from nothing more than collard greens, butter beans, corn pudding, and biscuits. The proverbial vegetable plate is commonplace in homes, diners, roadside hole-in-the-walls, even fine-dining restaurants—but don't let the name fool you, because this isn't "vegetarian" food at all. Real-deal Southern vegetable dishes are often infused with a ham hock, smoked turkey wing, slug of fatback, or spoonful of pure bacon grease.

When I was growing up, our family made meals entirely from vegetables at least once a week. Not only were these suppers inexpensive to create, with many of the ingredients coming straight from the garden, but most recipes could be whipped up with little effort. There was always some sort of nonmeat, high-protein item, such as brown pinto beans cooked all day with a piece of salted fatback (page 86). Alongside, we might have a wedge of buttered cornbread or spoonbread (page 91), which is a lighter, more soufflé-like version of traditional cornbread. And there always had to be some kind of greens and maybe a bowl full of creamed new potatoes (page 81). We'd wash it all down with a jug of syrupy sweet tea or maybe a glass of cold buttermilk. In many ways, this was our version of the "meat and three" meal—but minus the meat, which we didn't miss at all.

When it comes to slow cooking, the vegetable plate (also known as "beans and greens") could not be more fitting. Most Southerners cook these dishes in a deep cast-iron pot or Dutch oven with nothing more than some simple seasonings. Dinner might consist of collards, turnip greens, or creasy greens (watercress) slow simmered all afternoon with nothing but a piece of seasoning meat and a dash of cider vinegar. Or there might be a meal made from "soup beans," with navy beans or pintos cooked with a piece of salt pork and a little cayenne pepper.

While I highly suggest not skipping the meat used in these dishes, you may have dietary concerns or simply prefer a vegetarian meal. In that case, compensate by adding other seasonings and aromatics, such as garlic, onions, tomatoes, cayenne pepper, or paprika. You can also add a little vegetable stock to your greens for flavor and to keep them fully vegetarian.

At the end of this chapter, you'll find a few breakfast and brunch ideas thrown in for good measure. Not surprisingly, many breakfast dishes cook beautifully in the slow cooker, from eggy, cheesy casseroles (page 97) to creamy stone-ground grits (page 99), and there's nothing better than waking up in the morning to the sweet aroma of brown sugar oatmeal (page 95). Just fire up the coffee maker and dive right in.

Kale with Ham Hocks

While collard greens are often the slow-cooked greens of choice in the South, I grew up enjoying my mom's slow-cooked kale made with ham hocks, bacon drippings, and sautéed onions. Both the ham hocks and the bacon drippings give this dish its signature smoky flavor, so I recommend going whole hog here. However, you may substitute olive oil or vegetable oil for the bacon drippings, if desired. Either way, be sure to drink up a shot or two of "pot-likker," the liquid left in the pot, because it's full of valuable nutrients. Garnish your greens with a sprinkling or two of hot sauce and cider vinegar and serve with a bowl of brown beans and cornbread for a real country-style meal.

Serves 6 to 8

1 meaty smoked ham hock, or 4 or 5 ham hock slices (about 8 ounces)

1½ cups water

1 cup chicken broth, low sodium or homemade (page 122)

12 cups torn fresh kale leaves, tough ribs and stems discarded (2-inch pieces)

2 tablespoons bacon grease, vegetable oil, or olive oil

1 onion, thinly sliced

⅛ teaspoon cayenne pepper, or to taste

2 tablespoons apple cider vinegar, plus more to serve

Salt and black pepper

Hot sauce, for serving

Put the ham hock into a microwavable bowl and cover with the water and chicken broth. Cover and microwave on high for 3 minutes, or until bubbly.

Spray the inside of the slow cooker with cooking spray, then add the greens to the slow cooker.

Heat a large pan on the stovetop over medium-high heat and add the bacon drippings. Add the onion and sauté until translucent and lightly browned, 5 to 7 minutes. Add the onions to the slow cooker. Then, pour in the ham hock mixture and stir.

Cover and cook on low for 6 to 8 hours, until your greens are nice and tender.

Remove the ham hock from the slow cooker and shred the lean meat. Return the meat to the pot, discarding the skin and bones. Add the cayenne, cider vinegar, salt, and pepper, then stir. Set the cooker to warm and serve straight from the pot alongside a bottle of your favorite hot sauce and extra cider vinegar.

The Spring Tonic My grandmother was a firm believer in the medicinal qualities of the spring tonic, a mountain tradition involving boiling spring greens and herbs such as sassafras, dandelion greens, pokeweed, creasy greens, or ramps in water, after which the remaining liquid would be strained off and drunk like a tea. This potent (and often foul-tasting) concoction was widely believed to function as a blood booster.

Shiny Pole Beans

Pole beans are long, heirloom-style fresh beans that are staked so they grow right up the pole, sometimes upwards of ten feet. Certain varieties are found in mountainous areas throughout Southern Appalachia during the summer months, including Cutshorts, Greasy Beans, and Kentucky Blue's. These regional beans boast a unique flavor that is prized by many, and their long, tough pods are made for cooking low and slow (they are also excellent for canning). This recipe is how my Granny Boohler back in Bluefield, West Virginia, cooked her pole beans, and she called them shiny, since after cooking them for hours with a piece of fatback, they developed a certain sheen. When it comes to cooking time, you can count on 3 hours total in the slow cooker. After that, it's up to you, depending on the style of beans you prefer. Down-home Southerners (as well as my granny) tend to go for softer, almost mushy-style beans. In that case, cook your beans in the pot another hour or longer. If you prefer more al dente–style beans, go ahead and serve them up after 3 hours. Serve with Country–Style Pork Ribs (page 60) and creamed potatoes (page 81) for Sunday supper. • If you can't find pole beans, you can substitute snap beans, but they will require less cooking time.

Serves 8

8 cups pole beans, trimmed and strings removed
1 cup water
1 (1- to 1½-inch square) piece fatback or salt pork
Salt and black pepper
1 teaspoon sugar (optional)

Spray the inside of the slow cooker with cooking spray.

Combine the beans and ¾ cup of the water in the slow cooker. Rinse any salt from the fatback under cold, running water and place it in a microwaveable container with the remaining ¼ cup water. Microwave on high for 1 minute. Add the fatback and liquid to the slow cooker and stir.

Cover and cook on high for 1 hour. Then decrease the setting to low and cook for 2 more hours, or until you've achieved your desired tenderness. Once the beans are done, season with salt and pepper and add sugar, if you desire a slightly sweeter bean. (Note: If you decide to add sugar, cook an additional 15 minutes.)

Remove the fatback and serve.

Nannie's New Potatoes in Cream Gravy

My Great-Nannie Charity lived in a small coal mining town deep in the mountains near Welch, West Virginia, where she was known to readily offer a home-cooked meal to any hard-working, hungry coal miners who needed a little something to eat. Like so many living in the coalfields, she cooked hearty, rib-sticking dishes with ingredients she already had on hand since grocery stores were both scarce and pricey. This is her recipe for new potatoes slow-cooked in a rich, cream gravy. A little goes a long way with this decadent side dish, and it's one that can sustain even the hungriest of table guests. For the full coalfield experience, I recommend serving the potatoes with a slab of meatloaf (page 46) and side of slow-cooked kale (page 78).

Serves 6 to 8

16 to 20 walnut-size new potatoes
 (red skin or tan skin)
1 teaspoon salt, plus more to taste
1 cup chilled whole milk
2 heaping tablespoons all-purpose
 flour
1 cup half-and-half
3 tablespoons unsalted butter, cut
 into small pieces
Black pepper
Fresh minced parsley, for garnish

Spray the inside of the slow cooker with cooking spray.

Scrub the potatoes but leave the skin on. Place the potatoes in the slow cooker and pour in enough warm water to barely cover. Add the salt. Cover and cook on low for 4 to 5 hours, until the potatoes are fork-tender. Drain the potatoes, reserving 1 cup of the potato water. Return the potatoes and the reserved potato water to the slow cooker.

In a large microwavable bowl, whisk together the cold milk with the flour until smooth. Add the half-and-half and butter. Cover and cook on high in the microwave until the liquid comes to a simmer, 3 to 4 minutes. Stir it and add it to the slow cooker, mixing it with the potatoes. Set the lid slightly ajar (you can prop it up on some rolled up paper towels) so it vents. Turn the slow cooker to high and cook until the sauce thickens, about 45 minutes. Season to taste with salt and pepper, the more black pepper the better. Mash some of the potatoes with a potato masher or a fork to make the sauce as thick as you like it. Transfer the potatoes to a serving bowl and sprinkle with parsley.

Cabbage and Stewed Tomatoes

When it comes to slow cooking, it doesn't get any easier than this recipe for cabbage and stewed tomatoes accented with spices and just a skosh of bacon drippings for flavor. Serve this side dish with pinto beans (page 86), fried apples, and a wedge of cornbread (page 124) for a true down-home mountain-style meal.

Serves 8

1 head green cabbage (about 8 cups), cored and cut into 2-inch pieces

1 cup sliced onion

2 (14.5-ounce) cans stewed tomatoes

1 (10.75-ounce) can condensed tomato soup

1½ teaspoons bacon grease or vegetable oil

1 tablespoon dried parsley

1 tablespoon dried Italian seasoning

2 teaspoons granulated chicken bouillon

½ teaspoon celery seeds

¼ teaspoon ground black pepper

⅛ teaspoon cayenne pepper

Salt

Spray your slow cooker with cooking spray. Combine the cabbage, onion, stewed tomatoes, tomato soup, bacon grease, parsley, Italian seasoning, chicken bouillon, celery seeds, black pepper, and cayenne in a large mixing bowl and stir well. Add the mixture to the slow cooker. Cover and cook on low for 6 to 8 hours, until the cabbage is tender. Season with salt and serve.

Mom's Creamy Corn Pudding

There wasn't a holiday meal in our house that didn't have at least one casserole dish filled with creamy corn pudding on the table. This recipe, created by my mom, is one of the best out there. Boasting a blend of creamed corn and canned corn, combined with rich half-and-half, eggs, sugar, vanilla, and nutmeg, this easy, economical pudding is almost as much a dessert as it is a side dish. Serve your pudding alongside Herbed Turkey with Corn-bread Dressing (page 72) for a festive slow-cooker dinner. • It's easy for this dish to become overly soggy, so I suggest you top the slow cooker with several layers of paper towels before covering it with its lid. This helps to absorb any excess moisture. (You may need to replace the paper towels as they soak with condensation, and this will lengthen your cooking time by as much as 20 minutes, since the slow cooker lid will be lifted.) Another tip: Line the slow cooker with parchment paper sprayed with cooking spray before adding the pudding mixture to make it easy to remove the pudding for table presentation.

Serves 6 to 8

1 cup half-and-half
⅓ cup all-purpose flour
2 (15-ounce) cans creamed corn
1 (15-ounce) canned corn, drained
2 tablespoons melted unsalted butter
2 tablespoons sugar
1 teaspoon vanilla extract
½ teaspoon salt, plus more to taste
¼ teaspoon ground nutmeg
Black pepper
3 large eggs, beaten

Generously spray the inside of the slow cooker with cooking spray.

In a large bowl, whisk together the half-and-half and flour, removing any lumps. Add both types of corn, the melted butter, sugar, vanilla, salt, and nutmeg. Season to taste with salt and black pepper. Add the eggs and stir to combine. Pour the corn pudding into the slow cooker and then fold over several thick layers of paper towels and lay these over the insert. Cover with the lid and cook on low for at least 6 hours and up to 7 hours, until the pudding has almost set.

During the last 30 to 45 minutes, remove the lid, crank the slow cooker up to high, and continue to cook until the pudding sets in the middle and the edges are browned. Your pudding is done when the center is set or a toothpick inserted in the middle comes out clean.

Serve the pudding straight from the slow cooker or remove with the parchment paper and place the pudding in a serving dish.

Sausage-Stuffed Acorn Squash

A traditional sausage stuffing made with bread crumbs, egg, and walnuts often ends up inside a turkey, but this stuffing goes into two pieces of hollowed-out acorn squash. This dish is heavy on the sausage, so it can easily be a meal all by itself or it can be served as an accompaniment to turkey or chicken. Depending on the size of your acorn squash as well as the size of your slow cooker, you may be able to fit only one acorn squash into the insert, in which case you should halve the stuffing recipe. When divided into halves or thirds, one squash should be enough to feed two or three people. Serve as a side or a main dish with a green salad and rolls.

Serves 4 to 8

2 acorn squash
1 teaspoon olive oil
1 pound sage breakfast sausage
½ cup chopped onion
1 clove garlic, minced
½ cup plain dried bread crumbs
¼ cup chopped walnuts
1 egg, beaten
¼ teaspoon salt
⅛ teaspoon black pepper
¼ cup unsulfured light molasses
½ cup apple cider

Slice off the stem ends of the squash and scoop out the seeds. Slice off a small piece from the bottom of the squash, so it will sit level in your slow cooker. Brush the edges and insides of the acorn squash with the olive oil.

In a sauté pan over medium-high heat on the stovetop, crumble and brown the sausage, about 7 to 8 minutes, or until crispy and cooked through. Use a slotted spoon to transfer the sausage to a large bowl. Remove half of the fat drippings from the sauté pan and discard. Cook the onion and garlic in the remaining drippings over medium heat until softened, about 5 to 7 minutes. Add the onion and garlic to the bowl. Mix in the bread crumbs, walnuts, and egg. Mix in the salt and pepper. Fill the squash with the sausage mixture.

Cut a piece of heavy-duty aluminum foil large enough to fit the inside of your slow cooker all the way up the sides and spray with cooking spray. Place the squash cut-side up on the foil (but don't wrap the foil around the squash) and brush the exposed flesh with the molasses. Pour the cider around the squash pieces. Cover and cook on low for 6 hours.

Remove the squash to a cutting board by lifting it up by the foil, and cut each squash into halves or quarters.

Black-Eyed Peas and Stewed Tomatoes

Bring a little prosperity to your dinner table this New Year by serving up a big bowl of black-eyed peas and stewed tomatoes. While beans in general are quite common in down-home Southern cooking, black-eyed peas have a special place in our hearts. They are thought to bring considerable luck, even wealth, especially when eaten on New Year's. Be sure to save your ham bone from the Dr. Pepper Roasted Sorghum Ham recipe (page 54) to flavor your beans. For a complete meal, serve the beans with spoonbread (page 91) and kale (page 78).

Serves 8 to 10

1 pound dried black-eyed peas (about 2 cups)

1½ teaspoons bacon grease or unsalted butter

1½ cups chopped onions

½ cup chopped green bell pepper

4 cloves garlic, chopped

2 (14.5-ounce) cans stewed tomatoes, drained

4 cups chicken broth, low sodium or homemade (page 122)

2 bay leaves

1 teaspoon brown sugar

1 teaspoon cider vinegar

½ teaspoon dried thyme

Pinch of cayenne pepper

1 leftover ham bone or meaty ham hock

Salt and black pepper

Minced sweet onions, green onions (both white and green parts), or chives, for garnish

Rinse and pick through the beans, then place them in a large bowl. Cover the beans with water by at least 2 inches and soak them overnight. Rinse and drain the beans.

Heat a cast-iron or sauté pan on the stovetop over medium-high heat and add the bacon grease. Add the onions, green pepper, and garlic and sauté for a couple of minutes, until translucent. Remove from the heat and set aside.

Spray the inside of the slow cooker with cooking spray. Add the beans, canned tomatoes, chicken broth, bay leaves, brown sugar, cider vinegar, thyme, and cayenne. Pour in the onion and pepper mixture along with any drippings. Nestle the ham bone into the beans.

Cover and cook on low for 9 to 11 hours, until your beans are tender.

Season the beans with salt and pepper (be sure to taste the beans first so you don't oversalt, especially if you are using a salty ham hock). Remove any meat from the ham bone and return to the beans. Discard the bone and the bay leaves. To create a creamier texture, mash up some of the beans against the sides of the slow cooker with a fork.

Spoon the beans into bowls and top with minced onions.

TO DRINK A Bavarian-style beer, such as Spoetzl Brewery's Shiner Bock from Texas

Hide a shiny penny in the pot of black-eyed peas just before serving. By tradition, the person who finds the penny in their bowl of peas will receive the most luck for the following year. Just be sure no one actually eats the penny—this is arguably not the best fate.

Orange Sorghum Sweet Potatoes
WITH CORNFLAKE TOPPING

When I first conceived this recipe, I imagined a steaming bowl of crunchily topped, orange-flavored sweet potatoes on the Thanksgiving table next to the turkey. Then I tried this dish topped with ice cream, and I discovered it also makes one heck of a tasty dessert. Feel free to serve these tangy, cornflake-topped sweet potatoes any way you like them, either as a side dish or warm with melted ice cream or whipped cream. If you've got a crowd coming over, this recipe doubles easily, so no worries there. While the sorghum syrup is what makes this dish truly shine, if it's not available where you live, feel free to substitute light molasses, honey, or cane syrup. • If you wish to transfer the sweet potatoes to a separate bowl for serving, line the inside of your slow cooker with parchment paper, so the paper just reaches over the rim. This way, you can easily lift the contents out of the cooker to transfer to a serving bowl.

Serves 4

2 tablespoons unsalted butter

2 pounds sweet potatoes, peeled and cubed into a 1-inch dice (about 5 cups)

¼ cup firmly packed brown sugar

¼ cup sorghum syrup, unsulfured light molasses, honey, or cane syrup

¼ teaspoon grated orange zest

2 tablespoons fresh orange juice

½ teaspoon ground cinnamon

¼ teaspoon salt

Pinch of cayenne pepper

TOPPING

3 tablespoons unsalted butter

⅔ cup firmly packed brown sugar

⅔ cup chopped pecans

⅔ cup cornflakes

Rub the inside of your slow cooker generously with 1 tablespoon of the butter. Add the sweet potatoes.

In a small bowl, mix together the brown sugar, sorghum, orange zest, orange juice, cinnamon, salt, and cayenne. Pour this over the sweet potatoes and mix well (I just toss everything with my hands). Dot the sweet potato mixture with the remaining 1 tablespoon of butter.

Cover and cook on low for 4 to 6 hours, until the potatoes are soft.

To make the topping, in a small saucepan, melt the butter and brown sugar until the sugar dissolves. Mix in the pecans and cornflakes. Sprinkle this mixture over the sweet potatoes and serve.

Country Ham and Egg Breakfast Bread
RED-EYE STYLE

This savory bread pudding combines all the elements of a classic country breakfast—eggs, country ham, coffee, and toast. Southerners are fond of red-eye gravy, a delicious sauce made from pork drippings and brewed coffee. This recipe nods to the red-eye tradition with a healthy dose of black coffee used to deglaze the pan in which the ham is cooked. This fluffy, all-in-one brunch-style dish layers sliced bread with eggs, cheddar cheese, and salt-cured country ham bits fried with black coffee—so all you'll need is more coffee (or a mimosa if you're feeling sassy) to make this a complete meal. • This recipe will cook in 2½ to 3½ hours, depending on how hot your slow cooker runs, as well as its size. If you start it early in the morning, you will be eating by brunch time. However, this is one of those recipes where you really need to keep the slow cooker lid closed; opening it can add as much as 20 minutes to the final cooking time. One final note: Don't add salt to this recipe since the ham is already quite salty.

Serves 6 to 8

¼ teaspoon bacon grease or
    unsalted butter
8 ounces country ham, such as
    Benton's Smoky Mountain, Edwards
    of Surrey, Virginia, or Smithfield,
    cut into cubes
¼ cup strong brewed black coffee
Generous pinch of brown sugar
8 to 10 (½-inch-thick) slices hearty
    white bread (preferably day-old)
2 cups grated sharp cheddar cheese
1¾ cups milk
10 eggs, beaten
Pinch of dry mustard powder
Black pepper

Preheat a cast-iron pan on the stovetop over medium heat. Add the bacon grease and when it begins to sizzle, add the ham. Sauté until just crispy, about 4 to 5 minutes. Pour in the coffee and add a pinch of brown sugar. Stir well, scraping up the bits off the bottom of the pan. Set aside to cool.

Generously spray in the inside of the slow cooker with cooking spray. Place a layer of bread on the bottom (you may need to cut some slices in half to make them fit) and then top with about half the ham and cheese. Repeat with another layer of bread, then top with the remaining ham and cheese. Pour any remaining pan juices over the top.

Whisk together the milk, eggs, dry mustard, and pepper in a bowl. Pour this mixture over the bread layers, pushing down on the bread if necessary so everything is submerged in the milk mixture. Cover and cook on low for at least 2½ hours and up to 3½ hours, or until puffy and fully cooked through.

Cut into slices and serve warm.

Sausage and Tater Tot Brunch Casserole

To this day, I still cannot resist a plateful of crispy tater tots, and this recipe takes the tot experience to another level by topping them with layers of breakfast sausage and a cheesy egg mixture before cooking the whole shebang in the slow cooker. Equally tasty as an afternoon brunch or an early Sunday supper, this rich, eggy casserole-style dish is a self-contained meal. • This is a high-volume recipe, so it works best in a 5-quart or larger slow cooker. If you need to use a smaller slow cooker, I suggest halving the recipe.

Serves 8

1 pound ground breakfast sausage

3 to 4 cups frozen tater tots, or enough to cover the bottom of your slow cooker

12 eggs

1¼ cups milk

Pinch of dry mustard powder

Pinch of salt

¼ teaspoon black pepper

1½ cups grated sharp cheddar cheese

¼ cup minced green onions (both green and white parts)

Preheat a large pan on the stovetop over medium-high heat. Crumble in the sausage and cook for 7 to 8 minutes, or until crispy and fully cooked through. Drain the sausage on paper towels.

Generously spray the inside of the slow cooker with cooking spray. Spread the frozen tater tots in the slow cooker, followed by the sausage.

Whisk together the eggs, milk, mustard, salt, and pepper in a large bowl. Add the cheese and onions. Mix well. Pour the egg mixture over the sausage and tater tots.

Cover and cook on low for at least 4 hours and up to 5 hours, or until the eggs are fully set. I recommend keeping an eye on it during the last hour or so of cooking—especially if your slow cooker tends to run hot—to make sure the edges don't burn. Serve straight from the slow cooker.

Creamy Cheesy Grits

Whenever I ask someone if they like grits, I get one of two answers: a resounding, "You bet!" or a head shaking, "I just don't like them." Never have I seen an ingredient inspire such dichotomous responses. The key to making grits that will turn grit haters into lovers is to use stone-ground grits instead of instant (which are precooked and dehydrated and tend to resemble porridge) and to season, season, season since grits on their own tend to be bland. This recipe forgoes the usual breakfast-style grits cooked in water and simply seasoned with butter by slow cooking them in chicken stock with butter. Once the grits are cooked, cheddar cheese and half-and-half are swirled in to create a savory, decadent dish that in no way resembles mushy cafeteria-style grits. • You can find stone-ground grits at many health food and specialty food stores and via the Internet. Serve grits with fried eggs, breakfast apples (page 94), bacon or sausage, and biscuits (page 123). I reccomend using a 4- or 5-quart slow cooker for this recipe—any larger and the grits risk drying out.

Serves 4 to 6

1 cup chicken broth, low sodium or homemade (page 122)

3 cups water

1 cup stone-ground grits, either white or yellow corn (not instant grits)

2 tablespoons unsalted butter

¼ teaspoon salt, plus more to taste

¼ teaspoon black pepper, plus more to taste

¼ cup half-and-half

½ cup grated sharp cheddar cheese, plus more for topping

Salt and pepper

OPTIONAL TOPPINGS

Cooked and crumbled bacon

Fried eggs

Fresh minced chives

Extra butter

Hot sauce

Generously spray the inside of the slow cooker with cooking spray. Pour in the chicken broth and water and whisk in the grits. Let sit for 5 minutes. Skim off any debris that floats to the top (this is known as the chaff). Add the butter, salt, and black pepper. Cover and cook on high for at least 2 and up to 3 hours, stirring once halfway through the cooking process.

Once the grits have reached your desired consistency, uncover and whisk in the half-and-half and cheese. Season with additional salt and pepper to taste. Cover and continue cook on low until the cheese is melted, 5 to 10 minutes. If the grits are too thick, thin with a little water, chicken broth, or additional half-and-half. Serve with your desired toppings.

CHAPTER FOUR

Desserts and Sweets

Slow-Cooker Desserts Done Up the Southern Way

Yes, you can make mouth-watering desserts in the slow cooker. From cakes and cobblers to cheesecakes and bread puddings, you can slow cook them the all-natural way (no cake mixes or canned pie filling here!) using fresh ingredients, just like grandma would.

Fruits do exceptionally well in the slow cooker because it allows their natural sugars to slowly break down and caramelize in a way that rivals traditional oven baking. In general, slow-cooked desserts are denser and boast rich, moist flavors. Delectable slow-cooked sweets like cheesecake and bread pudding fluff up beautifully when steam-cooked at a low heat, and basic cakes, from chocolate to gingerbread, always come out decadently moist and spongy.

It goes without saying that Southerners take their sweets very seriously, and we are proudly responsible for producing some of the best stuff out there: Red velvet cake, pecan pie, fried apple pies, banana pudding, and fried beignets are just a few of our sweet contributions. Moreover, desserts play an important role in our community. We are quick to contribute our best of the best to an already overflowing dessert table at family reunions, potlucks, community bake sales, and church potlucks. And we get pretty darned upset if you don't take a taste, so you better come hungry and be prepared to do plenty of "oohing and ahhing" because we'll be watching your reactions closely.

At no time are sweets more important in the South than when a family member or friend has lost a loved one. We turn to our best recipes in times of trouble— and many of our cake, pie, pudding, and gelatin salad recipes have been handed down for generations. These cherished recipes provide comfort and are often easy to make with ingredients we already have on hand in the kitchen (think flour, eggs, and sugar). There's something innately reassuring when someone knocks at your door, maybe even someone you don't know very well, and the first thing they do is hand you a freshly baked cake. Words often fail us, but cakes, cobblers, and puddings speak volumes.

In this chapter, I've adapted several of my family's favorites for the slow cooker. Several recipes suggest using a baking dish set inside the slow cooker insert; I've found that unless you use a very small slow cooker (say a 3½-quart capacity one), the cake batter spreads out too thinly and the cake dries out. A baking dish *inside* the slow cooker solves this problem.

Many of these recipes are considered prized family heirlooms, so the first time I tried them in the slow cooker, I just closed the lid, crossed my fingers, and hoped for the best. I'm happy to report that these desserts are as good as any I've baked in the oven (some even better). I think my grannies would indeed be proud.

Buttermilk Chocolate Spice Cake

This is a very old family recipe that has all of the elements of what makes a homemade cake truly decadent: lots of chocolate. And, this is no ordinary chocolate cake. This one is infused with cinnamon and cloves and gets a unique tang from the addition of buttermilk. Serve the cake with vanilla ice cream topped with a drizzle of caramel sauce (page 119) for the ultimate sugary explosion. • This recipe also involves baking the cake in a dish placed inside the slow cooker insert. I've found that a 1½-quart rectangular baking dish set inside a 6-quart slow cooker works best (and a 6 x 8-inch dish fits perfectly). Pouring the batter directly into the slow cooker results in a dried-out, slightly burned cake.

Serves 4 to 6

¼ cup unsalted butter, softened
¼ cup vegetable shortening
1 cup white sugar
1 egg, beaten
1 teaspoon vanilla extract
1 cup all-purpose flour
2 tablespoons unsweetened cocoa
1 teaspoon baking soda
¼ teaspoon ground cloves
¼ teaspoon ground cinnamon
¼ teaspoon salt
¾ cup buttermilk

ICING

¼ cup unsalted butter
¼ cup unsweetened cocoa powder
1 cup confectioners' sugar, plus more
    as needed, sifted
¼ cup whole milk or half-and-half
½ teaspoon vanilla extract

Line the bottom of the baking dish with parchment paper and spray it with cooking spray. In a large bowl, cream together the butter, shortening, and white sugar and beat until fluffy. Add the egg and vanilla and beat well. In a separate bowl, mix together the flour, cocoa, baking soda, cloves, cinnamon, and salt.

Add the dry ingredients in thirds, alternating with the buttermilk, to the sugar mixture. Mix well until combined. Pour the batter into the prepared baking dish and place it inside the slow cooker. Thickly layer several paper towels over the top of the slow cooker to absorb any evaporation.

Cover the slow cooker with the lid and cook on high for 1½ to 2½ hours, until a knife inserted into the center of the cake comes out clean. (Keep in mind that the cake will continue to cook once it's removed from the slow cooker, so don't overcook it.) Place the dish on a cooling rack for 10 minutes. Then, carefully flip the cake onto the rack and remove the parchment paper. Let cool before icing.

To make the icing, melt the butter in a saucepan over medium heat and stir in the cocoa. Take it off the heat and alternately add confectioners' sugar and milk, mixing it until smooth. Stir in the vanilla. If a thicker icing is desired, add additional confectioners' sugar and let cool a bit before frosting the cake. Spread the frosting over the top of the cooled cake.

Gingersnap Peach Upside-Down Cake

Fresh peaches are synonymous with Southern cooking, from jams and jelly to homemade peach pie topped with peach ice cream. This slow cooker dessert recipe combines all of the elements that make a traditional upside-down cake so irresistible—a rich, buttery cake layer and a gooey, sugary topping. Instead of the usual pineapple, I've substituted fresh peaches, and instead of nuts, I've crumbled tangy gingersnap cookies.

Serves 6 to 8

4 to 5 cups peeled and sliced fresh peaches (5 or 6 peaches)
¼ cup finely chopped crystallized ginger
¼ cup unsalted butter, plus 2 tablespoons, softened
¾ cup firmly packed brown sugar
1 cup crushed gingersnap cookies (8 to 12 cookies)
⅔ cup white sugar
2 tablespoons vegetable shortening
1 egg
1 egg yolk
½ teaspoon vanilla extract
1 cup all-purpose flour
1 teaspoon baking powder
½ teaspoon salt
½ cup half-and-half
Whipped cream or vanilla ice cream, to serve

Line the slow cooker with a large sheet of parchment paper, letting the ends reach over the rim, and pushing the paper firmly into the bottom of the slow cooker insert. Generously spray the parchment paper with cooking spray.

In a large bowl, combine the peaches and crystallized ginger. Set aside.

In a small saucepan on the stovetop over medium heat, melt ¼ cup of the butter. Stir in the brown sugar. Pour this mixture into the slow cooker and spread evenly over the bottom. Next, spoon the peach and crystallized ginger mixture over the butter mixture. Do not stir. Then sprinkle with the gingersnap cookie crumbs.

Use a hand-held mixer to cream together the white sugar, shortening, and the remaining 2 tablespoons of softened butter in a bowl. Add the egg, egg yolk, and vanilla and mix in. In a separate bowl, combine the flour, baking powder, and salt. Alternate adding the flour mixture and the half-and-half to the creamed sugar mixture. Mix well and spoon on top of the gingersnap layer, spreading the mixture a bit, but not mixing it. Everything should be layered.

Place several layers of paper towels over the slow cooker and replace the lid. Turn the slow cooker to high and cook for 1½ to 2 hours, until a knife inserted into the middle comes out clean.

Remove the lid from the slow cooker and cook an additional 15 to 20 minutes for the top to form a crust.

Lift the cake from the slow cooker using the long ends of the parchment paper and place on a large dinner plate. Place a second dinner plate on top. Holding both plates, carefully flip it over and remove the parchment paper. Slice the cake and serve topped with freshly whipped cream or vanilla ice cream.

continued

Gingersnap Peach Upside-Down Cake, continued

TO DRINK *Five-Spice Bourbon Cider*

Cocktail guru and food writer Autumn Giles strikes again with this warm-you-from-the-inside-out bourbon and cider combo, but this is no ordinary two-part drink. A hefty mix of winter-inspired herbs and spices (like star anise) make this the perfect drink for a chilly day. It's easy to double (or quadruple!) this recipe to serve more than one person. *Serves 1*

1½ fluid ounces good-quality bourbon
¼ teaspoon whole black peppercorns
½ cinnamon stick, plus more for garnish
¼ teaspoon whole fennel seeds
½ teaspoon (about 10) whole cloves
1 whole pod star anise
1 cup apple cider

Pour the bourbon into a small mug and set aside. Combine the peppercorns, cinnamon stick, fennel seed, cloves, and star anise in a spice grinder or mortar and pestle. Grind very coarsely, leaving some large pieces. You want the mixture to be coarse enough to easily strain out later.

In a small saucepan on the stovetop, heat the apple cider and the ground spice mixture over high heat, bringing it just to a boil. Immediately decrease the heat to low, simmer for 5 minutes, and remove from heat. Pour the cider mixture through a fine-mesh sieve directly into the mug with the bourbon. Garnish with a cinnamon stick.

Granny's No-Egg Applesauce Cake

This is a very old family recipe for applesauce cake. Densely rich and redolent with apples, raisins, nuts, and spices, this no-egg cake is made for breakfast and goes well with a hot cup of coffee. Black walnuts make an appearance, giving the cake a flavorful and uniquely Southern punch. • Because this recipe makes quite a large cake, I suggest using a 6-quart or larger slow cooker. On the other hand, the recipe can be cut in half and cooked in a 3½-quart or 4-quart slow cooker; just adjust the cooking time to 2 to 2½ hours. If you end up with leftovers, don't bother storing the cake in the refrigerator. Instead, store any leftover cake in an airtight container in a cool place, such as a basement, with sliced apples or oranges in the container to keep it moist for up to 2 weeks. Be sure to replace the fruit twice a week.

Serves 15 to 20

3 cups unsweetened applesauce

1 cup vegetable shortening

2 cups sugar

1 teaspoon vanilla extract

4 cups all-purpose flour

2 teaspoon ground cinnamon

1 teaspoon ground cloves

1 teaspoon ground nutmeg

½ teaspoon salt

1 cup dark raisins

1 cup golden raisins

1 cup pecans, chopped

1 cup black walnuts, chopped
   (or substitute English walnuts)

4 teaspoons baking soda

Line the interior of a 6-quart or larger slow cooker with a sheet of parchment paper (or aluminum foil). Push the paper firmly into the bottom of the insert, letting the rest of the paper come up the sides to reach over the rim. Spray the parchment paper well with cooking spray.

Put the applesauce in a small saucepan on the stovetop over medium-low heat and bring to a slow simmer.

Meanwhile, in a large bowl, cream together the shortening and sugar with a hand mixer, beating until fluffy. Mix in the vanilla. In another bowl, combine the flour, cinnamon, cloves, nutmeg, and salt. In another small bowl, toss the raisins and nuts with 2 tablespoons of the flour-spice mixture.

Stir the baking soda into the hot applesauce and add this to the shortening mixture in thirds, alternating with the dry ingredients. Beat well after each addition. Mix well and then add the raisins and nuts.

Ladle the batter into the prepared insert and place a thick layer of paper towels over the top of the slow cooker. Replace the lid and cook on high for 3 to 3½ hours or until the cake begins to pull away from the sides of the insert.

When the cake is done (the center may still be a tad soft), remove the lid and turn off the cooker. Allow the cake to rest inside the slow cooker for 15 minutes. Once a toothpick inserted into the center of the cake comes out clean, lift the cake using the parchment paper and place on a cooling rack. Let cool and carefully remove the parchment paper. Cut into slices and serve.

Chocolate and Caramel Black Walnut Candies

Here's a chocolate candy recipe that's inspired by chocolate turtles, but I've given it a bit of a twist by including strongly flavored black walnuts instead of English walnuts (you can substitute regular walnuts if desired). Bite into one of these delicate candies to reveal an ooey gooey caramel center that's impossible to resist. This recipe makes a lot of candies, so they are perfect for handing out as Christmas gifts, hostess gifts, or for garnishing a holiday buffet table. You can cut this recipe in half. Store leftover candies in an airtight container for up to 2 weeks or freeze. To make the recipe, you will need 140 bonbon size (1-inch) baking cups.

Makes 120 to 140 pieces

2 pounds dark or milk chocolate candy-coating discs
1 cup chopped black walnuts (or substitute whole pecans or English walnuts)
Caramel Sauce (page 119), chilled
2 ounces vanilla candy-coating discs (optional)

Spread out 70 bonbon cups on a large baking sheet.

Melt one-quarter of the chocolate candy-coating discs according to package directions. Using a measuring spoon, place a scant ½ teaspoon of melted chocolate in the bottom of each cup. Gently push 5 to 6 walnuts pieces (or one whole pecan or English walnut) into the softened chocolate. Finish a couple of rows at a time, melting more chocolate as necessary.

Add a rounded ¼ teaspoon of the chilled caramel on top of the nuts. Finally, cover the caramel layer with another ½ teaspoon of melted chocolate. Your candy should have four layers: chocolate, nuts, caramel, and chocolate. Repeat this process with the remaining bonbon cups and ingredients.

Melt vanilla candy coating discs according to package directions and drizzle over each candy, if desired.

Chocolate-Banana Cheesecake in Jars

These individual cheesecakes are as whimsical as they are tasty. Combining the best of two dessert worlds—creamy cheesecake and Southern-style banana pudding—this recipe raises the flavor notch by adding a crust of chocolate wafers. Make these cheesecakes a day ahead for best results because the flavors truly come together after being chilled overnight in the fridge. And before you start, make sure the six half-pint jars fit in your slow cooker insert!

Serves 6

1 cup chocolate wafer crumbs

1 tablespoon sugar

3 tablespoons unsalted butter, melted

16 ounces cream cheese, softened

2 eggs

1 (14-ounce) can sweetened condensed milk

1 teaspoon vanilla extract

1 large banana, cut into thin slices, plus additional sliced bananas for garnish

Whipped cream, for garnish

Shaved dark chocolate, for garnish

In a small bowl, mix together the crushed chocolate wafers, sugar, and melted butter. Partially fill six half-pint canning jars with about 3 tablespoons of this mixture, being sure to distribute it evenly. Set aside any leftover chocolate crust mixture.

In a large mixing bowl, using a hand mixer, beat the cream cheese until fluffy. Add the eggs, one by one, still beating the mixture. Pour in the condensed milk and the vanilla and continue to beat.

Fill each jar with about 1½ to 2 inches of the cream cheese mixture. Add an even layer of banana slices along with some of the reserved chocolate crust. Finally fill each jar with more cheesecake mixture, leaving about an inch of headspace. Lay a kitchen towel on the bottom of the slow cooker to protect the ceramic surface and place the uncovered jars in the slow cooker insert, making sure they are not touching each other or the sides of the cooker.

Fill a tea kettle with water and heat to just boiling. Pour just enough water into the slow cooker to come halfway up the glass jars. Cover the top of the slow cooker with several thick sheets of paper towels to absorb additional moisture. Cover the slow cooker and cook on high for 1 to 2 hours, until the cheesecakes begin to pull away from the sides of the jars. Using a pair of tongs, carefully transfer the jars (they will be very hot) to a wire rack. Cool completely. Screw on the lids and place the cheesecakes in the fridge until well chilled, at least 4 hours, but preferably overnight.

Just before serving, top each jar of cake with additional sliced bananas, a dollop of whipped cream, and shaved chocolate. Serve the cakes straight from the jars with spoons.

> To crush the chocolate wafers, pulse them in a food processor or add them to a resealable plastic bag and crush them with the back of a large spoon.

Lemon Blueberry Buckle

Whether you like to call them crumbles, slumps, or cobblers, there's nothing like the combination of fresh fruit, sugary batter, and citrus, and this blueberry buckle fits the bill. Unlike cobblers (which have a biscuit topping) or crumbles (which have a crispy, crumbly topping), buckles are made with the fruit nestled right into a cakey batter. Traditionally, these fruity desserts were baked in a heated cast-iron skillet, which gave them a lovely crispy outer crust. Make this rich dessert even richer by drizzling a quick and easy homemade lemon glaze over it just before serving. I suggest using a 5- or 6-quart slow cooker for this dessert.

Serves 6 to 8

3 tablespoons unsalted butter, softened
⅔ cup white sugar
2 tablespoons vegetable shortening
2 eggs
½ teaspoon lemon extract
1 tablespoon finely grated lemon zest
1 cup all-purpose flour
1 teaspoon baking powder
½ teaspoon salt
½ cup half-and-half

TOPPING
1 cup blueberries
2 tablespoons finely grated lemon zest
¼ cup firmly packed brown sugar

LEMON GLAZE (OPTIONAL)
2 tablespoons fresh lemon juice
1 tablespoon lemon zest
1½ tablespoons confectioners' sugar
1 tablespoon milk

Line a large slow cooker with a sheet of parchment paper, pushing the paper firmly into the bottom of the insert and letting the two cut ends reach over the rim. Turn the slow cooker to high, add 1 tablespoon of the butter and replace the lid.

Meanwhile, in a large bowl, cream the white sugar with the remaining 2 tablespoons of butter and the shortening. Add the eggs, one at a time, and mix until fluffy. Mix in the lemon extract and the lemon zest.

In a separate bowl, combine the flour, baking powder, and salt. Add this mixture, alternating with the half-and-half, to the creamed sugar mixture. Stir well and then spoon the mixture over the melted butter in the slow cooker, gently spreading it out (do not stir).

To make the topping, toss together blueberries, lemon zest, and brown sugar. Spoon this mixture evenly over the batter. Pile several thick layers of paper towels over the slow cooker and replace the lid. Cook on high for 1 to 2 hours, until a knife inserted into the center of the buckle comes out clean. Then turn the slow cooker to low, remove the lid and the paper towels, and allow the buckle to cook for another 30 minutes.

While the buckle is cooking, prepare the glaze. In a small bowl, whisk together lemon juice, lemon zest, confectioners' sugar, and milk. If the glaze is too thick, add a bit more milk or lemon juice.

To serve, carefully lift the buckle from the slow cooker using the long ends of the parchment paper and invert it onto a cooling rack. Remove the parchment paper, drizzle with the lemon glaze, and cut into slices.

Ginger Ale–Baked Pears

Homemade desserts flavored with soda pop, such as lemon-lime soda cake or chocolate coca-cola cake, are about as Southern as you can get. For this recipe, whole pears are stuffed with black walnuts and raisins and get jazzed up with a combination of fizzy ginger ale and maple syrup before going into the slow cooker. What results are soft, naturally sweet pears that have just a hint of syrupy zing. Serve this dessert warm, drizzled with plenty of ginger ale syrup along with freshly whipped cream. • Use as many pears as will fit comfortably in your slow cooker.

Serves 4 to 6

4 large or 6 medium firm pears, such
    as Bosc or Bartlett
5 teaspoons raisins
5 teaspoons chopped black walnuts
    (or substitute English walnuts)
5 tablespoons brown sugar
1 teaspoon ground cinnamon
½ cup ginger ale
2 tablespoons real maple syrup

Peel the pears and slice about 1 inch off their tops. Slice off a small piece of the bottom of the pear, so it can sit flat in the slow cooker. Core the inside of the pears with a corer or small melon baller.

Spray the inside of the slow cooker with cooking spray or rub well with butter and place the pears, cored side up, inside the cooker.

Stuff each pear with equal parts raisins and walnuts. Mix together the brown sugar and cinnamon in a bowl. Sprinkle about 2 teaspoons of the cinnamon-sugar mixture over and inside the pears. Pour the ginger ale and maple syrup into the bowl with the remaining cinnamon sugar and stir well. Pour this mixture all over the pears. Cover and cook for 4 to 5 hours on low until the pears are tender, but not so soft they fall apart. During the last hour, baste the pears a few times. The liquid should be syrupy. If it's too watery, turn the slow cooker up to high and set the lid ajar to allow some of the moisture to escape and cook until thickened.

Serve the pears in dessert bowls with whipped cream and any extra sauce.

CHAPTER FIVE

Southern Odds and Ends,
PLUS
Non–Slow Cooker Essentials

The Art of Preservation: Jams, Butters, and Stocks

Making your own spreads and condiments for preservation is a science, an art, and a cultural marker for real-deal Southern food and cooking. Food preservation, especially canning, drying, and freezing is an ancient tradition that is often passed from grandmother to mother to daughter, as it was in our house. I remember spending many Sunday afternoons in the kitchen with my mom snapping beans and slicing cucumbers and taking my turn stirring a big pot of slow-cooked apple butter. I can never forget the endless brightly colored rows of bread and butter pickles, shucked corn, and stewed tomatoes that lined my granny's basement walls. You could always find a jar or two of chow chow relish (page 87), a sweet relish made with peppers and onions, or a couple of containers of homemade apple butter (page 118) for topping savory pancakes or pork chops.

I grew up in a household with a full-on "waste not, want not" philosophy, especially when it came to anything from the garden or the produce stand. If Mom went to the farmers' market and saw a box of half-rotten peaches destined for the trash, she'd make an offer (usually a couple of bucks) for the whole lot, come home, and then spend the next several hours making a big batch of peach mango jam (page 121). Some of it would be canned, some would be frozen, but most of this chutney-like jam got slathered on biscuits or cornbread right on the spot.

To fully understand Southern cooking as it relates to preservation and avoiding waste, it's important to comprehend the notion of need. Too many families throughout the South have experienced some form poverty. Both sets of my grandparents grew up poor with one side of the family living and working in the West Virginia coalfields, an often brutal existence, especially during the thankless mountain winters, while the other half made do on a small plot of land up a hollow with a pig, a couple of chickens, a garden, and an outhouse. They wasted nothing because they couldn't afford to. Even scraps and bones found their use slow-simmered in a homemade stock. If it wasn't canned, dried, pickled, cured, or frozen, it was eaten fresh, and nearly everything harvested or slaughtered was used.

Of course, it's hard to enjoy treats like homemade preserves or apple butter without some homemade bread to slather it on. Southerners are known for their delicious baked goods—think buttery biscuits or warm-from-the-oven cornbread. I consider these to be Southern staples—but unfortunately, they tend not to work well in the slow cooker. So, I've cheated and included a few non–slow cooker essentials to round out your meals, including our family's recipe for lighter-than-air Angel Biscuits (page 123) and doughy homemade potato rolls (page 126).

A note about canning and preserving: Always follow the USDA's guidelines for safe canning, freezing, and refrigerating. Consult the USDA's website for additional information.

Peach Mango Jam

This recipe is for fruit jam made the old-fashioned way, but instead of standing over a hot stove and stirring it for hours, you can cook it in the slow cooker. As with many Southern jam recipes, the sweetness is up to you, so add additional sugar to taste or leave some out if you like it tart. Serve warm jam on a hot biscuit (page 123) or spread on toasted corn muffins. It's also excellent swirled into plain Greek yogurt or spooned over vanilla ice cream.

Makes 6 half-pint jars

8 cups peeled, pitted, and cubed firm, ripe peaches (7 to 8 peaches)
2 cups peeled, pitted, and cubed firm ripe mangoes (2 mangoes)
¼ cup fresh squeezed lemon juice
1 tablespoon unsalted butter
4 to 5 cups sugar

Spray the inside of the slow cooker with cooking spray. Mash half of the peaches and mangoes with a potato masher in a large bowl. Add the mashed fruit pulp and the remaining cubed fruit, lemon juice, and butter to the slow cooker. Stir in 3 cups of the sugar. Cover and cook on low for 3 hours.

Stir in the remaining 1 to 2 cups of the sugar, more or less depending on your taste. Remove the lid and cook on high for 3 hours, stirring every now and then.

Test for proper thickness by placing a small amount of jam on a cold saucer and putting it in the refrigerator to cool. The jam should have a viscous consistency, similar to honey, and not be watery. (Note that jam tends to get thicker after it sets for 24 hours.) If you want a thicker jam, then continue to cook it without the lid. The finished jam can be packed into hot sterilized jars and processed for 10 minutes in a boiling water bath according to the USDA canning instructions, or refrigerated.

Peeling peaches The easiest way to peel peaches is to score an "X" in the top of each fruit, submerge it in boiling water for 1 minute, and then immediately plunge it into an ice water bath until cool. After that, the skin should come right off.

Easy Chicken Broth

Once you start making your own chicken broth, you'll never go back to the canned stuff. Use cooked leftover bones and cartilage from a whole chicken (or from the Dry Mustard–Rubbed Shredded Chicken, page 69) for this one, and be sure to add in the cider vinegar, which helps to leach out additional minerals from the bones, primarily calcium. For extra seasoning, toss in some optional herbs, such as thyme, garlic, black peppercorns, and rosemary. For convenience, cook your stock overnight and then package it when you wake up.

Makes 8 cups

Leftover bones and cartilage
  from a whole cooked chicken
1 onion, quartered
1 cup coarsely chopped celery
1 cup coarsely chopped carrots
1 tablespoon cider vinegar
Optional herbs: whole sprigs of thyme
  or rosemary, whole black peppercorns, bay leaves, crushed garlic
5 cups water
Salt and black pepper

Put the chicken bones and cartilage in the slow cooker. Add the vegetables, vinegar, and herbs. Add the water; it should be enough to just cover everything. Cover and cook on low for at least 9 hours and up to 12 hours. Season with salt and pepper.

Strain the stock into a large bowl and let cool (discard vegetables, herbs, and bones). Skim off any fat and discard that. Pour into containers for freezing or glass jars for the fridge (just be sure to use the refrigerated stock within 3 days and frozen stock within 3 months).

Angel Biscuits

Here's a bread recipe that isn't cooked in a slow cooker but is just so good that I had to add it to the book. These biscuits earn their name because they rise high, all the way up to the heavens, due to the yeast and plenty of baking powder. While making biscuits with yeast is atypical in Southern cooking, once you bite into one of these airy, doughy gems, you just might be a convert. • A couple of biscuit making tips: (1) For optimal rise, be sure to make your biscuits in a warm kitchen; (2) When rolling out your dough, use as little additional flour as possible or the biscuits will be too dense; (3) Avoid twisting your biscuit cutter when cutting the dough. This causes the edges to pinch down, which can make your biscuits flat.

Makes about a dozen biscuits, depending on size

1 (¼-ounce) package active dry yeast (not instant yeast)
3 tablespoons very warm water (110°F to 115°F)
5 cups all-purpose flour
1 tablespoon baking powder
1 tablespoon sugar
1 teaspoon baking soda
1 teaspoon salt
1 cup cold vegetable shortening or unsalted butter
2 cups buttermilk
1 whisked egg white or 2 tablespoons melted unsalted butter
Salted butter, honey, jam, apple butter, or sorghum syrup, to serve

Preheat the oven to 400°F. Grease a large baking sheet.

Dissolve the yeast in the warm water in a small bowl. Let it stand for 15 minutes in a warm spot.

Meanwhile, sift together the flour, baking powder, sugar, baking soda, and salt in a large bowl. Cut in the shortening using two knives until you have small grains. Add the buttermilk and the yeast mixture and mix well. Turn onto a lightly floured board and knead gently for about a minute. If your dough is too sticky, add a little more flour.

Roll out the dough to a thickness of about 1 inch and cut out the biscuits with a biscuit cutter or the open end of a clean tin can. Brush the top of each biscuit with the egg white.

Bake for 12 to 15 minutes, or until the biscuits are golden brown on top. Serve hot, with butter, honey, jam, apple butter, or sorghum syrup.

Cornbread

This recipe isn't cooked in a slow cooker, either—but it's a Southern essential and a perfect side for many of the recipes in this book, so I just had to add it. Our family recipe incorporates stone-ground grits, giving the cornbread a bit of a crunchy texture. Also, this recipe is not very sweet. If you prefer a sweeter cornbread, feel free to add more sugar to the batter before baking. This cornbread is excellent sliced and pan-fried in butter in a cast-iron pan.

Serves 8

1 cup plain white stone-ground cornmeal (not instant)

¾ cup yellow self-rising cornbread mix

1 teaspoon sugar

½ teaspoon salt

¼ teaspoon baking soda

3 tablespoons sausage, bacon, country ham, or pork chop grease (vegetable shortening or half unsalted butter and half shortening will also work)

¼ cup plain white stone-ground grits

¾ cup water

1 egg

1 cup buttermilk

Salted butter, honey, sorghum syrup, or light or dark molasses, to serve

Preheat the oven to 475°F.

Sift the cornmeal, cornbread mix, sugar, salt, and baking soda into a large mixing bowl.

Add the fat drippings to a 9-inch cast-iron skillet and heat it in the oven until it starts to sizzle, about 5 to 7 minutes. Remove the pan from the oven and tilt the pan so the sides and bottom are well greased. Pour off and reserve 2 tablespoons of the grease.

In another bowl, mix the grits and water and microwave on high for 3 minutes. Stop and stir, then microwave again on high for 3 minutes and set aside. The grits will be about half done.

Whisk the egg in a small bowl and then whisk in buttermilk. Pour this mixture into the cornmeal mixture. Stir until the batter is well mixed but still a bit on the firm and dry side. Add the reserved pan drippings and grits. (If the grits and water have cooled, reheat for 30 seconds before adding.) Mix all of the ingredients well with a large spoon. Your batter shouldn't be too dry or too wet, but somewhere in between.

Pour the batter into the skillet and bake for 20 to 25 minutes, until a nice, golden brown crust has formed. Top with butter, honey, sorghum syrup, or molasses.

Potato Dinner Rolls

Bread is a must-have in the Southern kitchen, but unfortunately, most don't do well in the slow cooker. This recipe is for my mom's famous dinner rolls—they're a bit of work, but totally worth it.

Makes about 4 dozen rolls

1 (¼-ounce) package active dry yeast

½ teaspoon plus ½ cup sugar

½ cup warm water (110°F to 115°F)

1 cup peeled and chopped (large pieces) white potatoes

3 cups cold water

½ cup vegetable shortening

1 teaspoon salt

1 large egg

8 to 9 cups all-purpose flour

2 to 3 tablespoons unsalted butter, melted

In a small bowl, combine the yeast and ½ teaspoon of the sugar with the warm water and set aside for 15 to 20 minutes to allow the yeast mixture to get foamy.

Meanwhile, combine the potatoes with 3 cups of cold water and boil over medium-high heat, uncovered, until soft. Drain, saving the leftover cooking water; you should have about 2½ cups. If you have more than 2½ cups, boil the water a bit more to reduce. Let the water cool until it's just warm.

Combine the cooked potatoes with the 2½ cups potato water in a blender. Add the remaining ½ cup sugar, the shortening, and the salt and blend. Add the egg and blend for an additional 5 seconds.

Spoon the potato mixture into a large mixing bowl or stand mixer fitted with a dough hook. Add the yeast mixture and 5 cups of the flour; beat until smooth. Slowly add 3 to 4 additional cups of flour, ½ cup at a time, kneading after each addition until the dough is fairly stiff and smooth, but still a bit sticky. You may turn the dough onto a lightly floured surface if you find it easier to knead.

Put the dough in a large greased bowl. Cover the exposed surface of the dough with lightly greased plastic wrap, and then cover the plastic wrap with a moist kitchen towel. Refrigerate the dough for at least 8 hours. (Note: the dough will keep in the fridge for 5 to 6 days. Be sure to gently deflate dough at least once per day.)

When you are ready to make rolls, remove the dough from the refrigerator and gently deflate it on a lightly greased surface. Grease a 9-inch cake pan (for 9 to 10 rolls) or a 9 by 13-inch baking pan (for 18 to 21 rolls).

To form the dinner rolls, pinch off a ball of dough about the size of a large walnut, 1½ to 2 inches in diameter. Dip your fingers in the melted butter and gently shape into a smooth round ball. Place the dough ball in the prepared pan and continue forming balls, leaving about ½ inch space around each roll. When the pan is full, cover with greased plastic wrap and place in a warm area for the second rise. Re-cover any unused dough with plastic wrap and a damp towel and return to the refrigerator. Let the rolls rise in a warm spot for another 1½ hours or until they have doubled in size.

Preheat the oven to 350°F.

Remove the plastic wrap from the rolls and bake for 20 to 25 minutes, until golden brown. Remove the rolls from the oven and brush the tops with additional melted butter. Allow the rolls to set in the pan for a couple of minutes, then turn them out onto a cooling rack. Serve warm with butter. Store leftover rolls in an airtight container at room temperature.

Resources

More information on beverage suggestions

Abita Brewing Company
21084 Louisiana 36
Abita Springs, Louisiana
www.abita.com

Back Forty Beer Co.
200 North 6th Street
Gadsden, Alabama
www.backfortybeer.com

Barboursville Vineyards
17655 Winery Road
Barboursville, Virginia
www.barboursvillewine.net

Blenheim Vineyards
31 Blenheim Farm
Charlottesville, Virginia
www.blenheimvineyards.com

Broadbent Selections
15 South Sheppard Street
Richmond, Virginia
www.broadbent.com

Duck-Rabbit Craft Brewery
4519 West Pine Street
Farmville, North Carolina
www.duckrabbitbrewery.com

Foggy Ridge Cider
1328 Pineview Road
Dugspur, Virginia
www.foggyridgecider.com

Hanover Park Vineyards
1927 Courtney-Huntsville Road
Yadkinville, North Carolina
www.hanoverparkwines.com

Hardywood Park Brewery
2408 Ownby Lane
Richmond, Virginia
www.hardywood.com

King Family Vineyards
6550 Roseland Farm
Crozet, Virginia
www.kingfamilyvineyards.com

Lone Star Beer
San Antonio, Texas
www.lonestarbeer.com

Mountain State Brewing Company
54 Clay Street
Morgantown, West Virginia
www.mountainstatebrewing.com

New Orleans Lager & Ale (NOLA) Brewing
3001 Tchoupitoulas Street
New Orleans, Louisiana
www.nolabrewing.com

Pontchartrain Vineyards
81250 Old Military Road
Bush, Louisiana
www.pontchartrainvineyards.com

Prince Michel Vineyard and Winery
154 Winery Lane
Leon, Virginia
www.princemichel.com

Spoetzl Brewery (Shiner Bock)
603 East Brewery Street
Shiner, Texas
www.shiner.com

Smooth Ambler Spirits
745 Industrial Park Road
Maxwelton, West Virginia
www.smoothambler.com

Terrapin Beer Company
265 Newton Bridge Road
Athens, Georgia
www.terrapinbeer.com

Veritas Vineyard and Winery
151 Veritas Lane
Afton, Virginia
www.veritaswines.com

White Hall Vineyards
5190 Sugar Ridge Road
Crozet, Virginia
www.whitehallvineyards.com

Windy Hill Orchard and Cidery
1860 Black Highway
York, South Carolina
www.windyhillorchard.com

Index

Published in the United States by Ten Speed Press, an imprint of the Crown Publishing Group,
a division of Random House, Inc., New York.
www.crownpublishing.com
www.tenspeed.com

Ten Speed Press and the Ten Speed Press colophon are registered trademarks of Random House, Inc.

Library of Congress Cataloging-in-Publication Data
Morris, Kendra Bailey.
  The Southern slow cooker : big-flavor, low-fuss recipes for comfort food classics / Kendra Bailey Morris ;
photography by Erin Kunkel. — First edition.
      pages cm
1. Electric cooking, Slow.
2. Cooking, American — Southern style. 3. Comfort food. I. Title.
  TX827.M67 2013
  641.5975 — dc23
                          2013002067

Trade Paperback ISBN: 978-1-60774-512-9
eBook ISBN: 978-1-60774-513-6

Printed in China

Design by Sarah Adelman
Food styling by Katie Christ
Prop styling by Ethel Brennan

10 9 8 7 6 5 4 3 2 1

First Edition

More slow cooker cookbooks from Ten Speed Press

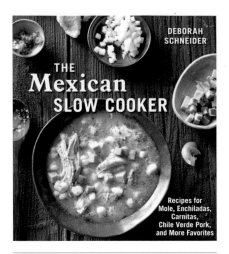

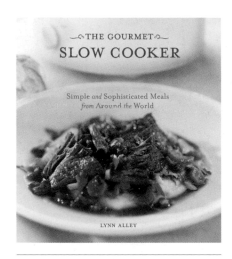

The Mexican Slow Cooker
Recipes for Mole, Enchiladas, Carnitas,
Chile Verde Pork, and More Favorites
Deborah Schneider
$19.99 (Canada: $23.99)
ISBN: 978-1-60774-316-3
eBook ISBN: 978-1-60774-317-0

The Gourmet Slow Cooker
Simple and Sophisticated Meals from Around
the World
Lynn Alley
$19.99 (Canada: $24.99)
ISBN: 978-1-58008-489-5
eBook ISBN: 978-1-60774-122-0

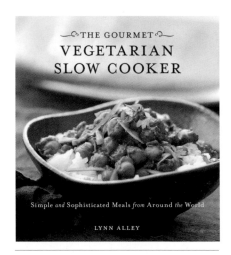

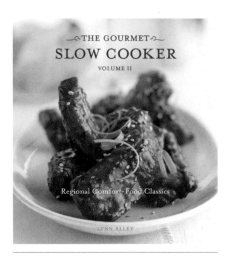

The Gourmet Vegetarian Slow Cooker
Simple and Sophisticated Meals from Around
the World
Lynn Alley
$19.99 (Canada: $24.99)
ISBN: 978-1-58008-074-3
eBook ISBN: 978-1-60774-085-8

The Gourmet Slow Cooker: Volume 2
Regional Comfort-Food Classics
Lynn Alley
$18.95 (Canada: $23.00)
ISBN: 978-1-58008-732-2
eBook ISBN: 978-1-60774-127-5